# NATURAL REVERBERATIONS

*This book is published with the financial assistance of CUSAT, Kochin-682022.*

# NATURAL REVERBERATIONS

VANI
PRITHVI

EDITOR
**PRABHAKARAN HEBBAR ILLATH**

Associate Professor of Hindi
Cochin University of Science and Technolgy (CUSAT)
P.O. Kochi University, Kerala-682022

Vani Book Company
An imprint of Vani Prakashan Group

Vani Book Company
An imprint of Vani Prakashan Group
*4695, 21-A, Daryaganj, New Delhi 110 002*
Phone: +91 11 23273167 Fax : +91 11 23275710
*India*
**Branches**
*Ashok Rajpath, Patna 800 004, Bihar*
*Coffee House Campus, Mahatma Gandhi Marg, Allahabad 211 001, Uttar Pradesh*
*Mahatma Gandhi International Hindi University, Wardha 442 001, Maharashtra*
*Goripur Taliya Para, 313, R.B.C. Road 24- Parganas (North) Kolkata 743 166, West Bengal*

Natural Reverberations
*Edited by* Prabhakaran Hebbar Illath

ISBN : 978-93-5518-231-9
Criticism/Environment


First Edition 2022

Price : ₹ 400



*Printed at R. Tek Offset Printers, Delhi-110 032*

*Vani Prakashan's signature motif is created by Artist Maqbool Fida Husain*

# Editor's Note

"Then a strange blight crept over the area and everything began to change. Some evil spell had settled on the community: mysterious maladies swept the flocks of chickens; the cattle and sheep sickened and died. Everywhere was a shadow of death." (Rachel Carson, The Silent Spring)

Historically, globalization has been an extension of imperialism. It is the aftermath of the development of industrialization that occurred together with the revolution in science and technology. The growth of private capital, profit making motive, market-oriented economy, industrialization, massive exploitation of human beings and the colossal depletion of natural resources are the consequences of the proliferation of the globalization. In this process humanitarian considerations, societal relations, creativity within individuals and the placental relation with nature are being lost. This disposition of human beings is critically termed as 'alienation' in Marxian terminology. In this alienated situation, the role of the human beings is limited to that of a consumer. In the post industrialized era, the growth of capital forces begins to challenge the very existence of life on earth. The 'terrorism of development' creates imbalances in all spheres of cosmos in the 'Capitalocene' ambience. As the poet said, 'death is everywhere, but the life is only on this earth.'

Contemporary literature, particularly poetry, in many languages, more or less, can be seen reflecting and reverberating the worries and woes of the human mind germinated out of our belligerent attitude towards nature. Poetry records the pathetic conditions of other biotic-abiotic elements on earth too. Kailas Vajpeyi notes with imaginative insight: 'If we kill a butterfly that will shut down the possibility the birth of a flower in this world. His poem declares thatall beings on the planet are dependent on one another… The dissociation from the wide web of relations of nature will result in the extinction of many life forms on earth. At this juncture, poetry raises an important question: how long can we survive in this world without pure water, without pure air? Can we create natural resources on demand? The poet tries to instill the feeling of humanity in the reader and makes a call to make the world more 'creative' in the true sense. In the era of multifaceted challenges, the poetry creates awareness that the 'divinity' (internal value) exists even in the tiniest microcosm of the universe. We all have to fly in this world like a butterfly, and we shall never allow anybody to turn this heaven of a planet into a hell. The whole of humanity has reached the brink of a monstrous disaster. Sambhoo Badalwrites: 'the nail of death/Piercing into my forehead/I cry, I bleed.'

Human beings are endowed with creativity, but to attain the material gains in life, we became insane. Rajiv K. Sinha once said- "Consumption has become a central pillar of life in the developed and industrialized nations and now even embedded in their social values and ethics of life." It is evident that humanity has to reframe the cultural paradigms of life at present. We have to adopt the ways of simplicity, reject the consumer culture and resist the slaughtering hands of capitalism. In the craving for wealth, the world is losing everything that assists us in sustenance. Hence Rajesh Joshisays- 'Adieu to suffocating poisonous smoke/Adieu to the venomous loneliness/Adieu to all Hullaballoo.'

There is very little to add. This collection of essays 'Natural Reverberations' seeks the ways and means to attain the 'bliss' of nature. It addresses different dimensions of green literature. I express my heartfelt gratitude to all the contributors. I wish to register a special thanks to the CUSAT and Vani Prakashan for undertaking the green project. Let me end this preface with a quote from William Blake which can serve as our motto: "To see a world in a grain of sand/And a heaven in a wild flower, /Hold infinity in the palm of your hand, /and eternity in an hour."

**–Prabhakaran Hebbar Illath**

# Contents

# Environmental Philosophy : An Introduction

**G. Madhusoodanan**

Humans have always learned to live with nature, because they recognized that it is the basis of their subsistence. Surviving and prospering in the diversity of habitats prevailing in the earth meant understanding the characteristics of each one of them. That was the beginning of thinking about nature. In ancient days such thinking was about cohabitation and coexistence. In the pre-religious world, it resulted in the worship of nature. Nature was the mother, the goddess for indigenous people around the world. Even after the advent of agriculture, a pastoral ethic prevailed. Ancient agricultural tools did not have the technological prowess to inflict any large-scale damage on the environment.

However, in those civilizations where agriculture was pushed to the limits, to increase production using major irrigation systems, collapse has occurred in the past. Human capacity for altering the environment, to the detriment of survival itself, began with the advent of industrial civilization. Modern machines, technology, fossil fuels and their widespread application for commercial benefit resulted in humans becoming agents of large-scale planetary transformations. That is why scientists have officially proposed in 2016 that 'Holocene', the geological age in which we live, should now be renamed as 'anthropocene'.[1]

## The Anthropocene

Preparations for this proposal for the renaming to 'anthropocene' had begun at the onset of the 21st century, in a paper published by Paul Crutzen.[2] Quoting the Italian geologist Antonio Stoppani (1873) Crutzen said that mankind has become "a new telluric force which in power and universality may be compared to the greater (natural) forces of earth." In 2007, Crutzen co-authored another study with other scientists including Will Steffen.[3] In that they declared: "The Anthropocene began around 1800 with the onset of industrialization, the central feature of which was the enormous expansion in the use of fossil fuels… Since then the human enterprise has experienced a remarkable explosion, the 'Great Acceleration', with significant consequences for earth system functioning… The 'Great Acceleration' is reaching criticality. Whatever unfolds, the next few decades will surely be a tipping point in the evolution of the Anthropocene." Many such studies followed and in 2016 it was decided to officially propose the renaming to the International Stratigraphy Commission. They are yet to officially approve it.

However, 'Anthropocene' has gained currency in scientific, cultural and literary fields.

Meanwhile some writers have opposed the 'Anthropocene' nomenclature, on the grounds that it bestows all responsibility for environmental destruction on a subjective and generalised category of 'humanity'. They argue that it was not humans as a whole who are responsible for the current predicament. The forces of capital have brought the planet and all life on it to the current predicament. Hence they have proposed naming our age as the 'Capitalocene'.[4] Semantics apart, the truth is that we are facing an unforeseen crisis of existence. Climate change has become an Orwellian nightmare. In this atmosphere, a universal cultural articulation of environmental philosophy has become imperative. Before examining the emergence and main tenets of ecophilosophy, it is relevant to examine its ancient and religious roots.

## Ancient and Religions Roots

As already mentioned, ancient humans across the globe, had the earth wisdom required for their survival. Sometimes such nature worship is referred to as 'paganism' which involved worshipping the pre-religious deities who were always rooted in land. The American environmental historian Donald Hughes has documented the eco-awareness in ancient civilizations, in an in-depth study.[5] In fact, in the face of the environmental crisis, paganism has re-emerged in the modern world. When religions emerged, even though they systematically destroyed pagan beliefs and symbols, many religious traditions absorbed much of the earth wisdom of the pagan days.

One of the most ancient and richest traditions of awareness of nature can be found in Hinduism, especially in the Vedas. The 'Prithvi Sukta' (Hymn to the Earth) in Chapter 12 of the Atharva Veda is the most evocative example of this rich Indian tradition. I wish to quote just two out of the 63 verses in the Sukta.[6]

> "May this Earth, whose
> surface undulates with
> many gradients, and
> sustains an abundant
> variety of herbs and plants
> of different potencies and
> qualities, support all human
> beings, in all their diversity
> of endowment, in mutually
> supportive harmony and
> prosperity" (Verse 2)
>
> "O' pure Earth, may that we
> utilise your soil well (for
> creative production)
> without causing you injury
> or harm and disturbing any
> vital element in you." (Verse 35)

Buddhism, Jainism and Sikhism, which are basically offshoots from Hinduism are also rich in nature wisdom. Buddhist wisdom is rooted in four divine abidings – love, compassion, spiritual joy and equanimity. Love and compassion involves compassion and care for nature also. It is about 'mindfulness' for all beings on earth. Joy involves experience of joy through contact with nature. In 'The Green Buddha', Christopher Titmuss makes this observation: "Time and again the Buddha referred to environmental life to illustrate a wise way of living. As we undergo transformation ourselves, so does the world in the way that we perceive and respond to it."[7] The Chinese philosophy of Taoism is also nature-centric in its world view.

The Judeo-Christian tradition is traditionally believed to be anthropocentric, emphasizing man's dominion over nature. In modern times, Lynn White Jr. reiterated this view in his 1967 essay 'The historical roots of our ecological crisis'.[8] White argued that the Judeo-Christian anthropocentrism stripped nature of its sacred status and exposed it to human exploitation and control. However, there has been a green tradition within Christianity, which is traced to St. Francis of Assissi and the 12$^{th}$ century German catholic nun and thinker Hildegard of Bingen. There have been many 'green' readings of the Bible. A 'green theology' has now become a rich branch of philosophy. In '*The Coming of the Cosmic Christ*', Matthew Fox makes this observation of the deterioration of the original Christian spirit while seeking a redemption from the patriarchal mindset to which it has succumbed: "what is needed if there is to be a twenty-first century for Mother earth and her children is a spiritual vision that prays, celebrates, and lives out the reality of the Cosmic Christ who lives and breathes in Jesus and in all God's children, in all the prophets of religions everywhere, in all creatures of the unvierse".[9] Islam, which grew out of Judaism and Christianity in the 7th century also has a vision of nature, especially strong in the Sufi tradition. Now we turn to the 'patron saints' of environmental thinking during the western post-enlightenment era.

## Patron Saints: Rousseau, Ruskin and Thoreau

Three thinkers of the eighteenth and nineteenth centuries who could be called the progenitors of modern ecological philosophy are Jean Jacques Rousseau (1712-1778) in France, John Ruskin (1819-1900) in England, and Henry David Thoreau (1817-1862) in America. Among the eighteenth century enlightenment philosophers, Rousseau was perhaps the only one who could be called the 'patron saint' of ecological thinking. His most important work '*A Discourse on the Origin of Inequality*' was published in 1754.[10] According to this thesis, the principal cause of the downfall of humanity was the system of private property. The development of civil society founded on the principle of private property, agriculture and industry led to the creation of authoritarian and hierarchical institutions. The discourse concludes with the contrast between 'noble savages' who lead vigorous and healthy lives in nature and modern man. Contrary to some misinterpretations, Rousseau's 'noble savage' concept is not about a return to primitivism, but about living in harmony with nature.

The lineage of John Ruskin's thought can be traced to two eighteenth century movements:

Romanticism and Evangelical Protestantism. Like the Romantics, he believed in the divinity of nature. Nature was a 'book of divine revelation'. But in later life, seeing that 'Mammon' replaced God, he lost his earlier conception of nature as the language of God. His vision transformed into a strong social consciousness, with the 1857 lectures which he called '*The Political Economy of Art*', but was later published as 'A Joy Forever.[11] He called for a society based on cooperation, not competition. It is also notable that he was a trenchant critic of J.S. Mill's capitalist thesis on the political economy. He turned from an art critic to a social critic. His 1862 book '*Unto this Last*' contained four essays which he called 'the first principles of political economy'.[12] In them he declared that 'there is no wealth, but life'. He denounced J.S. Mill's idea of 'the economic man'. For him the source of value is not 'gold', but light and water, the sources of life itself.

Henry David Thoreau was the archetypal 'philosopher of the wilderness'. Like his mentor Ralph Waldo Emerson, Thoreau was influenced by eastern traditions of thought. Thoreau's book '*Walden*' (1854) became popular in the environmental and cultural spheres.[13] His famous saying in the essay "Walking"– "In Wildness is the Preservation of the World" became the byline for wilderness enthusiasts and cultural anarchists.[14] As Roderick Nash said, "Wilderness in eastern thought, did not have an unholy or evil connotation, but was venerated as the symbol and even the very essence of society".[15] Thoreau though inspired by Emerson, moved away from Emersonian Christian transcendentalism. As Max Oelschlaeger says, "Emerson and the other transcendentalists unquestionably left their mark on Thoreau, but transcendentalism is a poor framework for understanding Thoreau's idea of wilderness.[16] Thoreau rejects the Cartesian-Newtonian paradigm, which has its origin in Christian ethics, when he writes, "The true man of science will know nature better by his finer organisation: he will smell, taste, see, hear, feel, better than other men. His will be a deeper and finer experience. We do not learn by inference and deduction and the application of mathematics to philosophy, but by direct intercourse and sympathy. It is with science as with ethics-we cannot know truth by contrivance and method; the Baconian is as false as any other". The conservationist and preservationist ethics which developed in the U.S., post-Thoreau through thinkers like Aldo Leopold, John Muir and George Perkins Mash owe their lineage to Thoreau's philosophy.

Much of the ecological literary criticism in the United States has its moorings in the Thoreauvian tradition. Thoreau is as much an artist as a naturalist. Thoreau's observations about what is relevant in literature- "in literature it is only the wild that attracts us"-rings a strong chord in the literary mind. Thoreau continues, "It is the uncivilized free and wild thinking in Hamlet and the Iliad, in all the scriptures and mythologies, not learned in the schools, that delights us. As the wild duck is more swift and beautiful than the tame, so is the wild-the mallard-thought… A truly good book is something as natural, and as unexpectedly and unaccountably fair and perfect, as a wild-flower discovered on the prairies of the West or in the jungles of the east."[17]

American eco-critic, Lawrence Buell, emphasize Thoreau's literary significance. Buell attributes Thoereau's canonization in America as a hero of high culture to his contemporary literary relevance. Buell says, "To read Thoreau in the light of his expanded conception of the environmental intertext is at once to redefine his cultural significance and to help revise our understanding of what counts as the American environmental imagination".[18]

## Gandhi and Ecophilosophy

An essay on environmental philosophy cannot be written without mentioning the guiding spirit of the Indian independence movement-Mahatma Gandhi who is venerated as the Father of the Nation. Gandhi's attitudes towards the materialistic, consumerist western culture were not only shaped by eastern philosophy; Gandhi with his western education, was the ideal product of an east-west symbiosis. More than external influences, Gandhi had tremendous intuitive knowledge, which is the source of his wisdom. Writings of Tolstoy, John Ruskin and Thoreau played a crucial role in shaping Gandhi's philosophy and strategy. Ruskin's rejection of 'economic man', his belief in the innate goodness of humans etc.. profoundly influenced Gandhi. Thoreaus' essay "On the Duty of Civil Disobedience" was a major political influence on Gandhi in shaping his vision of Satyagraha-the form of non-violent political resistance. Gandhi's economic vision of a decentralized village-oriented and nature-friendly development was also compatible with Thoreau's three famous maxims of life: "Simplicity, Simplicity, Simplicity." Thoreau's idea of civil disobedience lived on through Gandhi's

Satyagraha. In a resurgent, post-independent India, Gandhi's economic vision was relegated to the marginal alternative movements. The philosophical moorings of early Indian environmentalism were largely Gandhian.

He believed that western style industrialization was not suitable for India. Extreme industrialization and mass production was a recipe for perdition. Instead, he visualised a village-oriented decentralized system of 'production by masses'. In an article published in '*Harijan*' on 1st September 1946 titled 'The Curse of Industrialism' he clarified his vision thus: "I would categorically state my conviction that the mania for mass production is responsible for the world crisis. When production and consumption both become localised, the temptation to speed up production indefinitely and at any price disappears… Machinery has it place; it has come to stay. But it must not be allowed to displace necessary human labour… I refuse to be dazzled by the seeming triumph of machinery. I am uncompromisingly against all destructive machinery… At the same time, I believe that some key industries are necessary."[19]

In a world tormented by widespread ecological destruction and climate crisis, Gandhi's foresight rings true. In the 21st century, the world will have to move into an age where fossil fuel burning has stopped, rapacious mining has ceased to destroy vital ecological habitats, production is decentralized and where agriculture again becomes the mainstay of human civilization. Gandhi was not against industry per se; he was against the 'culture of industrialism' which he believed will ruin the world. Seventy-five years after he wrote the above quoted lines, the world is staring at the consequences he predicted.

There are a few other eco-philosophical theories like Gaia theory by James Lovelock. He visualises the earth as a living organism functioning in highly complex ways, through the natural cycles like bio-geochemical cycles. Paucity of time does not permit me to go into all such theories. Hence we will dwell briefly on four of the prominent ecophilosophies:

- Deep Ecology
- Environmental Ethics
- Ecofeminism and
- Ecosocialism.

## Deep Ecology

'Deep Ecology' entered the lexicon when the Norwegian philosopher Arne Naess published a paper which was to become the foundational text for this branch of ecophilosophy.[20] He made a distinction between the 'shallow ecology movement' and deep ecology movement. Shallow ecology is restricted to "the fight against pollution and resource depletion and is aimed at the health and affluence of people in the developed countries". He was making a distinction between 'first world' environmentalism and philosophical ecology, which he termed as 'ecosophy'. Naess laid down seven cardinal principles of a more comprehensive and holistic deep ecology as follows:

- Rejection of the man-in-environment image in favour of **a 'relational' and 'total field' image**. All living organisms are but knots in the biospherical net (the web of life) or the field of intrinsic relations.
- Recognising 'in principle' that human survival necessitates some killing, exploitation and suppression, he spoke of a **'biospherical egalitarianism'**. This involves a deep-seated respect or even veneration for ways and forms of life, conceding the 'equal right to live and blossom'. The anthropocentrism of modern civilization was rejected.
- **Principle of diversity and symbiosis**. It recognises that diversity enhances the possibility of survival, co-existence and richness of life forms. Its essence is a 'live and let live' principle rather than the antagonistic view of 'either you or me'.
- **Antic-class stance**. This follows from the earlier enunciated principles of biospherical egalitarianism and diversity. Does not recognise divisions based on class within countries or the segregation of 'developing' and 'developed' nations.
- **Fight against pollution and resource depletion**. While continuing this fight, ecologists should keep in mind the other principles enunciated here.
- **Complexity, not complication**. The astoundingly high level of complexity of living organisms, ways of life and biospherical interactions is

not fully comprehensible to humans and makes 'thinking in terms of vast systems' inevitable. This 'complexity-not-complication' precept **favours 'division of labour' and not fragmentation of labour**. It seeks "more sensitivity towards continuity and live traditions". In the realm of technology, it favours 'soft technique'.

- **Local autonomy and decentralization**. This promotes local material and mental 'self-sufficiency' and an autonomous decentralised local self-government to complement them.

Naess elaborated his vision into a book published in the Norwegian language in 1976. However, a translation of his work was available in book form in English only in 1989.[21] Even though his initial 1973 paper was inspired by ecology and systems theory, the further development of his ecosophy drew on a variety of philosophical and religious traditions like 'Native American' eco-wisdom, Zen Buddhism, Taoism, Gandhian thought and some European pre-socratic thinkers, besides Spinoza Thoreau and Aldo Leopold. After his 1973 paper, 'deep ecology' gained momentum in the late 1970s in the United States through the work of Bill Devall and George Sessions. '*Deep Ecology: Living as if nature mattered*' co-authored by them was published in 1985, before publication of Naess's book in English.[22] They followed Naess's footsteps and elaborated on many of the foundational concepts. After elaborating the fundamental precepts laid down by Naess, Devall and Sessions go on say that, "thus deep ecology goes beyond the so-called factual scientific level to the level of Self and Earth Wisdom."[23] Besides Devall and Sessions, the deep ecology movement spawned a number of thinkers in the United States, based on the plethora of traditions from which Naess drew his inspiration.

Outwardly much of what Naess said was in tune with the needs of the ecological movement. His fourth fundamental precept denies existing realities in a divided world. His sixth fundamental tenet of 'complexity, not complication' was criticised widely for being regressive in many respects. In concepts like 'division of labour', too much emphasis on 'continuity and traditions' echoes many conservative stereotypes. Also, the political neutrality espoused by deep ecologists is highly problematic when capitalism is moving towards extinction of life on earth, through the spectre of climate change. The frontal attack on anthropocentrism by deep ecologists like David Ehrenfeld, could ultimately become misanthropic and undermine critical human rights violations perpetrated in the name of infinite growth, by destroying pristine habitats and livelihoods.[24] The prominent European Philosopher Slavoz Zizek, points out the lack of philosophical clarity in deep ecology in a thought provoking essay, 'Of Cells and Selves'. Zizek says: "the paradox of Deep Ecology is that, in its very rejection of anthropocentrism, it charges man with the duty of subordinating the narrow interests of the human species to the interests of all other forms of life and of the entire biosphere. Does it not thereby elevate man into a kind of 'functionary of Life'?

One can only ask of man to sacrifice his narrow interests and take into account the interests of the whole of life if one conceives of him as a 'universal being'... Deep Ecology thus in no way escapes the charge of anthropocentrism".[25]

## Environmental Ethics

Like deep ecology, the vision of environmental ethics emerged from a multiplicity of native, religious traditions and modern philosophical thinking. Perhaps, a significant modern philosophical milestone was the philosophy of the seventeenth century Dutch-Jewish Philosopher Baruch Spinoza (1632-1677).[26] His ethics is derived from the teachings of Jewish Holy Scriptures Torah and Kabbalah. He reinterpreted Torah from the traditional book of law, history and ritual into a source of theistic inspiration. Spinoza viewed 'God as Nature' and said that ethics without metaphysics is meaningless. For him, God is not only the effecting cause of the existence of things, but also their essence. Arnae Naess has compared Spinoza's philosophy to Mahayana Buddhism. Spinoza negates the mind-body duality of Descartes. There is a certain amount of metaphysical determinism in his vision of nature. But his philosophy is much more complex and it is not appropriate to reduce him to a mystic, a reformed Jew or a Buddhist.

However, there is another completely divergent tradition of environmental ethics, as seen in the writings of the 19th century anarchist philosopher Peter Kropotkin (1842-1921). Born into an aristocratic princely Russian family, he later fled to England and spent most of his life there. Even though he believed in the oneness of nature, his philosophy was rooted in a mechanical explanation of all phenomena, embracing the whole of nature. His concept of nature extended to the life of human societies encompassing their economic, political and moral problems. He grounded human morality in an objective philosophy of nature. Morals were an outcome of the social needs and habits of humanity – metaphysics is not the source of morals. In his classic work on ethics, he proclaimed: "Nature has thus to be recognised as the first ethical teacher of man. The social instinct, innate in men as well as in all the social animals, – this is the origin of all ethical conceptions and all the subsequent development of morality."[27] He believed in human survival based on a system of communal mutual aid; a kind of radical communalism.[28] The thinking of Kropotkin can be assimilated into the 21st century vision of ecological socialism.

However, in the western countries, especially the United States, modern environmental ethics evolved from a Thoreauvian wilderness ethics, and the ethics of nature conservation and preservation as espoused by Aldo Leopold (Land Ethic) and John Muir. It should be remembered that the conservationists are more human centred, while the preservationists are nature-oriented. The conservationists are conservative and continue to perpetuate the ethic of domination and ownership. In the mid-1970s, two Australian philosophers began forefronting the philosophy of environmental ethics. In 1974 John Passmore published *'Man's Responsibility For Nature'*.[29] He presented an impassioned exposition of the philosophical and ethical problems faced by humanity as they exploit and modify the world around them. In 1975, another Australian philosopher, Peter Singer published *'Animal Liberation'*.[30] The focus was on the cruel treatment meted out to animals in modern farms, factories and kitchens. Thus the concept of animal liberation was conflated with a larger sphere of environmental ethics. In 1979, a new journal titled *'Environmental Ethics'* was published by Eugene C. Hargrove. Articles and research papers started pouring in. Deep ecology and environmental ethics, together, spawned a host of activist movements. The biggest drawback of these movements (except for those of conservationists) was an inherent misanthropy and nature mysticism. Very often, their 'holism' deny humans any separate autonomy.

They tend to espouse an extreme form of holism as elaborated by J. C. Smuts in 1926: Taking a plant or animal as a type of 'whole', we notice the fundamental holistic characters as a unity of parts which is so close and intense as to be more than a sum of its parts ... the whole and the parts therefore reciprocally influence and determine each other and appear more or less to merge their individual characteristics".[31] Smut proposed holism as a philosophical alternative to mechanism. Like plants and animals, human beings are also products of their environments, but they also in turn influence their environment. Applied at a societal level, such extreme holism can be a recipe for authoritarianism. The 'whole' may very well be greater than the sum of its parts, but that does not mean that the parts are insignificant or expendable. Environmental ethics is hardly 'holistic' in that as a philosophical position, it fails to address the complex environmental realities now facing the world.

## Ecofeminism

In modern ecological philosophy, ecofeminism emerged as an independent theory, as a forward evolution from the foundations of feminism. Mainstream western feminism was moving away from the problems of ordinary women. Germaine Greer in her later work '*The Whole Woman*' criticised western feminism for succumbing to consumerism. Perhaps Simon de Beauvoir was the first to think about women, in the context of nature in her work '*The Second Sex.*[32] The idea of economic development or growth had become a patriarchal project whereby men were overcoming women's immanence through masculine virtues of transcendence. Growth became a patriarchal project of subduing nature, creating an artificial duality between culture and nature. One critical observation of Beauvoir is that the patriarchal urge for growth has a psychological dimension also, beyond the economic dimension.

Ecofeminism emerged as a distinct ecophilosophical theory in French in 1974 in a study by French feminist Francoise d' Eaubonne who is also one of the founders of the ecology-feminism centre in 1972. Francoise was a member of the French Communist party for ten years. She was an activist, ecologist, feminist and opposed nuclear energy. Her essay 'The Time for Ecofeminism' was included in her French book '*Feminism or Death*' published in

1974. This was later translated into English by Ruth Hottell in 1994.[33] Francoise qualifies ecofeminism as "a new humanism born with the irreversible end of the male society". According to her, "at the base of the ecological problem are found the structure of a certain power" (patriarchal power). The patriarchal system has been the bane of the planet, ever since men arrogated to themselves the power to decide on the fertility of the soil and women. She views the capitalist system of profit as a creation of phallocracy and points out that even if the capitalist system is abolished, the patriarchy in the new system also resists all revisions of the established patriarchal order. She concludes her study with this observation. "(The phallocracy) is at the base of an order which can only assassinate nature in the name of profit if it is capitalist and in the name of progress if it is socialist".[34] Francoise recgonised the patriarchal politics implicit in conventional notions of economic growth, of the right and the left.

While Francoise was publishing her thesis in France, parallel developments were taking place in the United States. A very influential book titled '*New Woman, New Earth*' by Rosemary Radford Reuther was published there in 1975.[35] It articulated what could be called an 'Ecofeminist Theology' – a feminist version of liberation theology. Reuther says: "Women must see that there can be no liberation for them and no solution to the ecological crisis within a society whose fundamental model of relationships continues to be one of domination. They must unite the demands of the women's movement with those of the ecological movement to envision a radical reshaping of the basic socio-economic relations and the underlying values of this (modern industrial) society". The institute of social ecology in Vermont, established by Murray Bookchin held a seminar on ecofeminism in 1976. This event was coordinated by Ynestra King who later emerged as an ecofeminist philosopher by publishing the notable essay 'Feminism and the Revolt of Nature' in 1981.[36] She is known as the advocate of 'Social Ecofeminism'. Meanwhile two other influential books were published in the United States in 1978. One was *'Gyn-Ecology'* by Mary Daly, which was a feminist reinterpretation of the Bible.[37] The other book was *'Woman and Nature'* by Susan Griffin.[38] Both these authors can be called radical cultural ecofeminists. Another influential work published in USA in 1980 was 'The Death of Nature' by Carolyn Merchant, who is a let-of-centre ecofeminist.[39] In 1980 ecofeminism became a global movement with the organisation of the first ecofeminist conference, 'Women and Life on Earth: Ecofeminism in the Eighties', held at Amherst (Massachusetts) in the United States.

Suffice to say that ecofeminism is not a monolithic philosophical stream; there are different iterations of it, the lineage of which can be traced to the diversity of approaches in feminism. One such iteration is spiritual ecofeminism. Writers like Starhawk, Merlin Stone and Dolores La Chapelle point out that in the pre-patriarchal ancient society, women were held in esteem, to the point of being worshipped as female deities, like the Sacred Earth. Modern women can retrieve that stature by challenging the phallocratic technological civilization. The return of the female principle could become the focus of human unity and efforts to conserve nature. Dolores La Chapelle goes one step further in conflating women's sensuality, sexual energy and fertility as the basis for a new spirituality.[40] As already mentioned, social econofeminism articulated by writers like Ynestra King did not gain much popularity because Murray Bookchin's 'social ecology' was not widely received. Then there are liberal eco-feminists who believe in technological solutionism to mitigate environmental problems and in the creation of equal opportunities for women in the economic system.

Cultural ecofeminists believe that gender relations became skewed in favour of men, due to culturally constructed dominant patriarchal systems and power structures. Women were culturally painted as weak and biologically inferior to men. This argument was used to discriminate, exploit, subordinate and oppress women through religious, legal, institutional and even violent means. Similar was the case with nature and all forms of life therein. Cultural ecofeminists argue for revival of cultural norms, rituals etc., to rebuild human relationship with nature and simultaneously for women's liberation through political interventions. However, most traditional ecofeminisms believe in the ethics of care, interconnectedness, cultural transformations etc., while being mildly political.

Perhaps the most political of all the ecofeminisms is socialist ecofeminism. It evolved from the struggles and resistance movements of working class women in cities, rural areas and indigenous habitats, especially in the developing world. The lineage of socialist ecofeminism can be traced to socialist feminism. In capitalism, the majority of women from the oppressed classes don't even have access to the formal structures of the economic system and they are deprived of its 'trickle-down' benefits, if any. At the same time, the patriarchal structure has bestowed all responsibility of collecting the basic necessities of rural life like water, fire wood etc. on women. Hence environmental destruction makes life more miserable for them. They have to walk larger distances and slog for longer hours. That is why Mary Mellor qualifies socialist ecofeminism as a 'deep materialism.[41] Socialist ecofeminism emphasizes the fact that even in traditional socialist societies, the domestic labour of women is considered as having low or no exchange value. Further, it recognizes that exploitation has other dimensions beyond objectified labour, and hence gender discrimination is prevalent in the work place.

Another prominent socialist eco-feminist philosopher Ariel Salleh argues for redefining production, beyond the conventional socialist conceptions of 'conditions of production', to give a prominent place to women's labour within it.[42] Carolyn Merchant gives emphasis on redefining 'production' from the perspective of 'reproduction'.[43] The concept of 'reproduction' goes beyond biological reproduction of humans, to include the regenerative processes inherent in nature. For example, vegetative reproduction by plants, regeneration of vital resources like water or even social reproduction of ideas, norms and structures critical to social justice and harmony. Maria Mies and Vandana Shiva define socialist ecofeminism as a 'subsistence feminism', making it more relevant to millions of women in the developing world.[44] Socialist ecofeminism has now evolved into a full fledged 'Marxist Ecofeminsim', with the detailed theoretical work of writers like Pamela Odhi. She concludes the preface to her 2014 work *'Watersheds in Marxist Ecofeminism'*, with this quote from Mary Mellor: "the valued economy has gained in power and ascendancy through the marginalisation and exploitation of women, colonised peoples, waged labour and the natural world increasingly on a global scale".[45]

## Ecological Marxism or Ecosocialism

Contrary to the 20th century applications of the Marxian doctrine in countries ruled by left parties across the world and the conventional criticism of Marxism as a Promethean doctrinc, thc writings of Marx are rich in environmental insights. The evolution of his philosophy has its moorings in his early life. He got his doctorate in 1841 at the age of twenty three for the dissertation, "The Difference between the Democritean and Epicurean Philosophy of Nature". Epicurus who was born in 341 B.CE in the Greek island of Samos, put forth a materialist philosophy of nature by rejecting religious mysticism. Lucretius, the Roman poet, a follower of Epicurus, wrote a long poetic discourse, translated as "The Way Things Are' or 'On The Nature of Things' which is an early materialistic ecological treatise.

His doctoral thesis led the way to the later development of Marx's philosophy. John Bellamy Foster dwells in detail on the ecological significance of Epicurean thought and its influence on Marx.[46] After getting his doctorate, Marx began his professional life in 1842 as a journalist (and later editor) in the newspaper 'Rheinische Zeitung' published from his home province of Rhineland, in Prussia (former Germany). In 1842, the Rhineland provincial assembly was debating 'The law concerning the theft of wood' from private forests. This law was meant to criminalise the traditional rights of the rural community to collect dried wood and twigs, etc. from such forests. Marx who was by then the editor, wrote a series of articles in Rheinische Zeitung between 15 October and November 3, 1842.[47] These series of articles were Marx's first writings on the environmental question, and was based on an ecological vision rooted in the livelihood of the poor.

In other words, Marx considered nature as the material basis of human survival. Hence it behove on humans to protect and preserve nature not just for one generation, but for future generations. These sentences from Vol.3 of '*Capital*' clearly indicate this view: "Even as a whole society, a nation or even all simultaneously existing societies taken together, are not the owners of the globe. They are only its possessors, its usufructuaries and like *boni patres familias*, they must hand it down to succeeding generations in an improved condition".[48] His was a philosophy which combined a materialist conception of history with a materialist conception of nature. In fact, before Henry David Thoreau's nature mysticism, and Ernst Haeckel's pronouncement of the science of ecology, Marx had written on the materialist vision of ecological philosophy. The socialist states as they were founded in the 20th century lost sight of this critical aspect of Marx's thought. In the Soviet Union, there was a strong current within the Bolshevik movement to develop the new nation based on Marx's ecological vision. But with the ascent of Joseph Stalin to power, these ecosocialist visionaries were ignored, jailed or even eliminated.

However, in the second half of the twentieth century, thinkers again began to discover Marx's environmental vision. Alfred Schmidt, a student of the Frankfurt School philosopher Theodore Adorno, published *'The Concept of Nature in Marx'* in German in 1962 – the same year as the publication of Rachel Carson's canonical book *'The Silent Spring'*. This was later translated into English in 1971.[49] Even though this book contributed to interpreting Marx's ecological vision, its over-emphasis on the 'social construction of nature' led to depicting Marx as a proponent of productivism. Perhaps, the first clear elucidation of Marx's ecological thinking can be seen in the 1977 book *'Marx and Engels on Ecology'*, by Howard Parsons.[50] Ecological Marxism or Ecosocialism emerged in the 1980s as a distinct branch of philosophy. However, it should be emphasized that it is not a separate philosophical movement, but an elucidation and elaboration of ecological vision in Marx. So, before talking about the emergence of Ecosocialism, there is a need to survey Marx's own ecological vision.

Marx began his later philosophical journey by making Hegel's vision of nature stand on its head. Hegel spoke of the essential unity of Man and Nature – an abstract and metaphysical vision wherein nature directly influences world history. But in Marx's thought, nature influences history indirectly – through the medium of 'production'. Karl Korsch, in one of the best evocations of Marxist thought said that in Marx, "physical nature does not enter directly into history. It does so indirectly i.e. as a process of material production which occurs not only between man and nature, but at the same time between man and man."[51] This does not mean that capitalism's depredations on nature is in any way justified. Just that, for subsistence, humans need to have a 'metabolic relationship' with nature.

Marx had done in-depth studies of this metabolism, in the context of agriculture, through his researches into the scientific works of at least half a dozen scientists. Among them, he was most influenced by the work of Justus Von Liebig. What especially influenced Marx was Liebig's views on the 'robbery system' of capitalist agriculture, which leads to soil exhaustion endangering the subsistence of future generations. In chapter 15 of Capital Vol. I, Marx says: "all progress in capitalist agriculture is a progress in the art, not only of robbing the labourer, but of robbing the soil; all progress in increasing the fertility of the soil for a given time, is a progress towards ruining the lasting sources of that fertility."[52]

The same chapter of *'Capital'* also makes this crucial observation about capitalist growth:

"Capitalist production, by collecting the population in great (urban) centres, and causing an ever-increasing preponderance of town population, on the one hand concentrates the historical motive power of society; on the other hand, it disturbs the circulation of matter between man and the soil, i.e. prevents the return to the soil of its elements consumed by man in the form of food and clothing; it therefore violates the conditions necessary to lasting fertility of the soil". This creates a 'rift' in man's metabolism with nature. This has later been developed as the 'Theory of Metabolic Rift' by John Bellamy Foster – the pioneering ecosocialist thinker. These are not isolated sentences picked up from Marx's work; his entire body of work is rich in such environmental vision. This formed the basis for development of ecosocialism.

John Bellamy Foster classifies the development of ecosocialism into various stages, besides a 'prefigurative phase' prior to them.[53] The prefigurative phase emerged in consonance with the growth of the environmental movement in the 1960s and 1970s. Numerous socialist thinkers like Barry Commoner, Herbert Marcuse and Istvan Meszaros "saw ecological concerns as blending naturally with the fundamental historical-materialist critique emanating from Marx". The first stage of ecosocialism grew in the 1980s, with theoretical contributions from thinkers like James O'Connor, Ted Benton, Andre Gorz, Enrique Leff, etc. According to Foster, the first stage ecosocialism "proceeded to graft Green theory into Marxism". However, there was one distinct theoretical strand in the first stage which gained wide acceptance – the theory of 'Second Contradiction of Capitalism'.

The 'first contradiction' in Marxist theory is about the conflict between capitalist productive forces or the capitalists and the relations of productions or the labour class. James O' Connor, the Founder Editor of the theoretical journal *'Capitalism, Nature, Socialism' (CNS)* published his study on the 'Second Contradiction' in the journal in 1988, and later included it in his book on Ecological Marxism.[54] In the context of the ecological crisis, a new 'Second Contradiction' emerges in capitalism. In the 'Second Contradiction' conflict arises between the process of production and the 'Conditions of Production'. Out of the three main conditions of production enumerated in Marxism 'the external physical conditions' or the materials and resources extracted from nature is of prime importance. The destruction of nature due to this extractive process and the eventual depletion of these resources leads to an end of the capability of capitalism to continue growing. Environmental resistance led by 'new social movements' and conflicts became a feature of late capitalism. O' Connor says that there are not one but two paths to socialism – the first and the second. In a sense, the first stage involved criticism of Marx and Engels on their shortcomings.

The second stage can be said to have begun with the publication of two works at the twilight of the 20th century and the beginning of the 21st century. The 1999 book was *'Marx and Nature'* by Paul Burkett and the 2000 book was *'Marx's Ecology: Materialism and Nature'* by John Bellamy Foster.[55] Many other important thinkers like Elmar Altvater, Peter Dickens, Martin Empson, etc., are associated with this second stage. The second stage involved a rejection of the criticism of Marx and Engels by first stage thinkers and a rediscovery of the ecological depths of classical Marxist thought. Two main strands of thought in this stage was Foster's theory of the 'Metabolic Rift' and Altvater's theory of 'Fossil Capitalism'. The essence of metabolic rift theory was indicated earlier. 'Fossil Capitalism' is a further development of Marx's original thinking of the role of coal, a fossil fuel, in the growth of capitalism, amplified by the later spread and influence of another fossil fuel–oil in the 21st century. The Orwellian nightmare of climate change facing the planet and humanity today is the result of excessive $CO_2$ emissions from continued fossil fuel burning.

There are many other theoretical strands that have developed in ecosocialism. Also, beyond the prefigurative phase, first stage and second stage mentioned by J.B. Foster, there is now a third stage in ecosocialist theory. It actually involves exploration of how to apply ecosocialist thinking to solve practical problems. Otherwise it revolves around 'praxis'. In conclusion it can be said that ecosocialism is today a theoretically sound strand of ecophilosophy, with a large body of work developed from the 1970s onwards, but which began blooming fully with the onset of the twenty-first century. For those who wish to see a more pluralistic, humane just and democratic socialism emerge, ecosocialism offers great hope.

Ecophilosophy has influenced various branches of humanities and sciences like literature, sociology, psychology, anthropology, economics etc. Adherence to a particular branch of ecophilosophy is determined by the social and political predilections of each individual. In literature ecofiction, ecopoetry and ecological literary criticism (or ecocriticism) have grown phenomenally in the past two decades. Ecocriticism continues to grow and develop in diverse directions.

## References


1. Media Note: Anthropocene Working Group. Posted by ap507 on 29th August, 2016. www2.le.ac.uk.
2. Crutzen, Paul J.Geology of Mankind. Nature, Vol.415/ January 2002.www.nature.com.
3. Steffen, Will, Paul Crutzen et.al. The Anthropocene: Are Humans overwhelming the great forces of nature? Royal Swedish Academy of Sciences. Ambio.vol.36, no.8, December, 2007.
4. Moore, Jason W. (ed). Anthropocene or Capitalocene: Nature, History and the Crisis of Capitalism. Kairus (PM Press), Oakland (California), 2016.
5. Hughes, Donald J. Ecology in Ancient Civilizations. University of New Mexico Press, Albuquerque, 1975.
6. Sohoni, Shrinivas S. Hymn to the Earth: The Prithvi Sukta. Sterling Publishers Pvt Ltd., New Delhi, 1991.
7. Titmuss, Christopher. The Green Buddha. Insight Books, Devon (UK), 1995.
8. Lynn White, Jr. 'The Historical Roots of our Ecological Crisis'. 'Science', (155), 1967 pp.1203-7.
9. Fox, Matthew. The Coming of the Cosmic Christ. Harper Collins, San Francisco, 1988.
10. Rosseau, Jean Jacques. Discourse on the Origin of Inequality (1754). In Britannica Great Books of the Western World, Vol.35.
11. Ruskin, John. A Joy Forever (1857). E-book crated by Simplicissimus Book Farm, USA.
12. Ruskin, John (1862). Unto this Last and Other Writings. Penguin Classics, 1997 Edition.
13. Thoreau, Henry David (1854). Walden. The Modern Library, New York, 1950 Edition.
14. Thoreau, Henry David. The Natural History Essays. Peregrine Smith Books, Salt Lake City, 1980.
15. Nash Roderick. Wilderness and the American Mind. Yale University Press, New Haven, 1967.

16. Oelschlaeger, Max. The Idea of Wilderness. Yale University Press, New Haven, 1991.
17. Thoreau. Walking (In. Natural History Essays) op.cit.
18. Buell, Lawrence. The Environmental Imagination. Harvard University Press, Cambridge (MA), 1995.
19. Gandhi, M.K. The Curse of Industrialism. In India of My Dreams. Rajpal and Sons Delhi, 2013 Edition.
20. Naess, Arne (1973). 'The Shallow and the Deep, Long Range Ecology Movement: A summary'. Inquiry (16) pp. 95-100. In. (ed) George Sessions. Deep Ecology for the 21st century. Shambhala Publications, Boston, 1995.
21. Naess, Arne. Ecology, Community and Lifestyle: Outlines of an Ecosophy (Trans. David Rothenberg). Cambridge University Press, Cambridge, 1989.
22. Devall, Bill and George Sessions. Deep Ecology: Living As If Nature Mattered. Peregrine Smith Books, Salt Lake City, 1985.
23. Ibid.p.65.
24. Ehrenfeld, David. The Arrogance of Humanism. Oxford University Press, Oxford, 1978.
25. Zizek, Slavoz. Of cells and Selves. In, 'The Zizek Reader' (ed). Elizabeth Wright and Edmond Wright. Blackwell publishers, Oxford 1999.
26. Spinoza, Baruch. The Ethics of Spinoza: The Road to Inner Freedom. Citadel Press (Kensington Publishing Corp), New York, 1988 Edition. (Ed) Dagobert D.Runes.
27. Kropotkin, Peter (1922 Posthumous Original). Ethics: Origin and Development. Black Rose Books, Montreal, 1992 Edition.
28. Kropotkin, Peter (1902). Mutual Aid: A Factor of Evolution. A Reprint of the 1902 original by 'Forgotten Books'.
29. Passmore, John (1974). Man's responsibility for Nature: Ecological problems and Western Traditions. Scribner, New York, 2016 Edition.
30. Singer, Peter (1975). Animal Liberation. ECCO Press, 2001 Edition.
31. Smuts, Jan C. Holism and Evolution (1926). Literary Licensing, LLC. 2013 reprint.
32. Beauvoir, Simon de (1949 in French). The Second Sex. Vintage, London, 1997 Edition.
33. Eaubonne Francoise d'. The time for Ecofeminism (translated by Ruth Hottell). In Carolyn Merchant (ed), Ecology: Key concepts in Critical Theory. Rawat Publications, New Delhi, 1996.

34. All quotes from Ibid. pp.175, 185 and 194 respectively.
35. Reuther, Rosemary Radford. New Woman, New Earth. The seabury Press, New York, 1975.
36. King, Ynestra. Feminism and the Revolt of Nature. In Carolyn Merchant (ed), 1996 op.cit.
37. Daly, Mary. Gyn/Ecology. The Women's Press Ltd., London, 1979.
38. Griffin, Susan. Women and Nature (1978). The Women's Press Ltd., London, 1983 Edition.
39. Merchant, Carolyn. The Death of Nature.
40. Chapelle, Dolores, La. Sacred Land, Sacred Sex: Rupture of the Deep. Finn Hill Arts, Colorado, 1988.
41. Mellor, Marie. Breaking the Boundaries. Virago, 1992.
42. Salleh, Ariel. Ecofeminism as Politics. Zed Books, London, 1997.
43. Merchant, Carolyn. Earthcare: Women and the Environment. Routledge, New York, 1995.
44. Mies, Maria and Vandana Shiva. Ecofeminism. Zed Books, London, 2014.
45. Odih, Pamela. Watersheds in Marxist Ecofeminism. Cambridge Scholars Publishing, New Castle Upon Tyne (U.K.), 2014.
46. Foster,J.B. (2000). Materialism and Nature. Monthly Review Press, New York.
47. Marx, Karl. Debates on the Law on Theft of Wood. https://marxists.architexturez.net.
48. Marx, Karl. Capital Vol.III. Progress Publishers, Moscow, 1988 edition, p.776.
49. Schmidt, Alfred. The Concept of Nature in Marx. NLB Publishers, London, 1971.
50. Parsons, Howard L. Marx and Engels on Ecology. Greenwood Press, Connecticut, 1977.
51. Korsch, Karl. Karl Marx (1936). Hay Market Books, Chicago, 2017 reprint.
52. Marx, Karl. Capital Vol.I. Progress Publishers, Moscow, 1988 edition. pp.474-475.
53. Foster, J.B and Paul Burkett (2016). Marx and the Earth: An anti-critique. Haymarket Boos, Chicago, 2017 Edition.
54. O'Connor, James. The Second Contradiction of Capitalism. In, 'Natural Causes: Essays in Ecological Marxism'. The Guilford Press, New York, 1998. p.158-177.
55. (i) Burkett, Paul. Marx and Nature. Macmillan, London, 1999.

    (ii) Foster, J.B. Marx's Ecology: Materialism and Nature. Monthly Review Press, New York, 2000.

# Ecofeminism and Its Concerns

**Jancy James**

**Forester** : ***What do the forests bear ?***
*Profits , resin and timber*
**Women** (Chorus):***What do the forests bear ?***
*Soil, water and pure air,*
*Soil, water and pure air, Sustain the earth and all she bears.* (A poetic dialogue recited by the women of Chipko movement)

As a combination of the two terms-Ecology and Feminism- Ecofeminism is as much an environmental discourse of feminism as a feminist discourse of environmentalism. Ernst Haeckel the German biologist who coined the term ecology in the mid 19$^{th}$ century conceived it as a world view that accepted the totality of an organism with all organisms it comes into contact, both animate and inanimate, dispelling the Cartesian anthropocentric view of the human being as a subject privileged and destined to control and own the earth in its entirety as an object. Ecofeminism confronts and critiques the domination of men over nature and pleads for an egalitarian bonding negating the hierarchical structure of superiority of the human over nature as a dominable and consumable commodity.

Ecology came to be "popularised as a combined socio-economic and biological study in the 60's to examine how the human use of nature is causing pollution of soil, air and water, the destruction of the natural life system of plants and animals , threatening the base of life upon which the human community depends".[1] 'Deep Ecology' moves from a critique of the social and technological devastation of nature into the "symbolic psychological and cultural patterns by which the humans have distanced themselves from nature" and replaced themselves from as part of it to the ruler, possessor and dominator. Deep Ecology proposes an "ecological healing that will lead to a "psycho – cultural / spiritual conversion from the anthropocentric stance of separation and domination" into a "communion in nature through an interconnected community of life" (Rosemary Radford Rurther. 33)[2]

Feminism is an equally complex concept and practice that protests against the age-old domination of man over woman –patriarchy –and affirms the need and rights of women for a relationship of equality between man and woman. Ecofeminism views the relationship between human beings and nature and the relationship between man and woman as characterized by hegemony and exploitative use by a patriarchally oriented society. Both ecology and feminism indulge in a radical critique of the unjust domination, unequal separatism and merciless possessiveness prevailing in nature and in social life. The term Ecofeminism was coined by the French left wing thinker, ecologist and feminist Francoise d'Eaubone in 1974. She used it as a loaded term to describe a philosophical movement backed by a transformative politics. Ecofeminism considers ecological issues and feminist issues as well. It is 'deep ecology' and belongs to the third wave feminism. It is an environmentalism from the woman's perspective and experience - a mutual impregnation between environmentalism and feminism. Ecofeminism counters the sexist arrogance and unscrupulous invasiveness of the Baconic concept – "nature is a woman waiting to be raped"(Bacon)[3]. The anthropocentric and utilitarian attitude to nature is challenged by ecofeminism. It criticises the excessive importance given by modernism to rationality and development. An anti - mechanistic and anti-consumerist view that derides the present development rhetoric is a significant component of its epistemology. It opposes technomania which distances human beings from nature. The failure and unsustainability of the techno economic development model is evidenced by climate change, landslides, repeated unpredictable occurences of floods and global warming. Uncaring and irresponsible interventions in the life and continuity of nature rob the biosphere of its spontaneous growth and sustenance. What happens to nature because of the selfish and dominating forces of male political and economic power happens to women through misogyny and oppression. The paradigmatic link between the pervasive exploitation of environment and women by a hegemonic patriarchy constitutes the basic premise of ecofeminist discourse. "The Ecofeminists believe that women interact with the environment in a spiritual, nurturing and intuitive manner. As a result of women's close association with the environment, their domination and oppression has occurred in conjunction with the domination and degradation of the environment" (Brownneyn James, p.96)[4]. Women are not only the first victims of environmental deterioration but also play a key role in the defence of nature. Ecofeminism is the thought and praxis that addresses this double sided issue.

The western philosophy of dualism that separates humans and nature into two binaries is contested by ecofeminism. It calls for a holistic vision of human beings within environment, and a healthy egalitarian system of dynamic interrelatedness. In such a system women are also liberated from the subservient and exploited condition created by patriarchy that operates in every aspect of living including government, educational system, commerce, religion and family. Ecofeminism is a vision of restoration of the damaged ecosystems from an endangered world, simultaneously with the acquisition of freedom and dignity of the female self and the recognition of her power and relevance on a par with the male.

Ecofeminism disapproves the age old identification of the male with culture and woman with nature. It interrogates such a culture where apparent agents of development like reason, science, technology, mechanisation, urbanization etc. are wielded by a power structure dominated by men as authority and majority. The identification of woman with earth/ nature is caused due to several factors :

1. The cyclical nature of woman's physiology
2. The woman's close contact with nature because she is entrusted with the responsibility of nurturing the family, vis - a - vis cooking, gardening, housekeeping, farming, child-rearing, cleaning etc. So women are in greater need of natural resources than men.
3. A cultural belief that women have intuitive link with nature.
4. Biologically the right side of the brain which generates and guides emotions is more active in women whereas the left side of the brain which is identified with logical thinking, reasoning and analytical ability is more functional in men. Hence the various changes and fluctuations in the activities and expressions of nature are established as similar to the emotional faculty of women who pass through different stages of life, each loaded with associated feelings. For example, menstruation, wifehood , pregnancy, motherhood etc.
5. Women are affected the worst by environmental deterioration. Endangering the health of the earth through pollution and other plausible ways have the most harmful impact on woman's health and reproductive health.

There is a paradoxical dimension in the relationship between technology and women. Technology has contributed immensely to lessening the physical hardships of women by providing them with plenty of gadgets and facilities. Household utensils, transport facilities, communication tools and many more in this category have speeded up women's activities and made living easier for them. But only some classes of women in society are the benefactors of this advantage. Women in third world countries especially in Africa and the rural parts of India are ignored in this so called technological revolution. Technology has robbed the earth of its natural resources in a massive manner, making even the facilities that it has provided unsustainable. Human greed for amassing wealth has led to the exploitation of nature by using technology irresponsibly and unethically, which amounts to technomania. Both nature and women are losers in this development model which is the fabrication of male driven capitalist strategies. Ecofeminism, in projecting an ideological opposition to such a development discourse is inevitably socialist, anti-capitalist and anti-patriarchal. If strands of counter - development narrative, anti-modernist attitude and anti-rationality are found in ecofeminist concept it cannot be dismissed as baseless. Ecofeminism does indulge in the fight against all unsustainable progress, unethical development projects as well as the denial of equality and peace to women by destroying the wellness of the earth. Ecofeminists are Eco-warriors who are sensitive to the perverse side of unsustainable development brought about by the techno-economic race for material gain. They alert humanity about the paradigmatic link between the exploitation of environment and that of women by men. Ecofeminism asserts that all forms and structures of oppression are interconnected and that they should be countered as a totality. So the oppressive and exploitative domination of nature as well as woman by patriarchal power structures must be targeted together. Mindless colonialism which was exploitative in content and form exercised domination all over the world for centuries and established a greedy, utilitarian strategy of 'killing life for the sake of sap' -of cultures, peoples, land , nation, and consequently women. Its flawed politics continues in overt and covert ways, making every portion of the world a global market, and turning majority of the population into consumerists. Ecofeminism is a resistance to materialism which ignores the spirit and sustenance of the land with its animate and inanimate belongings. Materialistic techno-economic development models are inherently structured on

1. Hierarchy
2. Binaries
3. Hegemony
4. Exploitation

Patriarchial power is also functioning on these wheels. So in a world where decision–making, power and wealth are all monopolised by man, ecofeminism opposes the twin domination of women and nature by man. This mode of domination is rooted in the concept of nature and culture/development as binaries. Ecofeminism, both as theory and praxis, aims at uprooting this perception and replacing it with an integrative, inclusive and egalitarian vision that cuts down the barrier between nature and development, and holds them in a mutually empowering totality. In a world where masculine qualities of reason and rationalism are glorified to condemn feminine qualities of intuition, nurturing and caring, and where culture attempts to control and dominate nature, just as men universally control and dominate women, ecofeminism posits itself as a transformative force.

Ecofeminism has lent itself to an amazing plurality of discursive practices. As a liberative and transformative ideology it presents itself as a pragmatic, realistic and socialist dynamics in discourses that expose the condition of women deprived of basic amenities of life. The opening lines of *Longing for Running Water : Ecofeminism and Liberation* by Sister Yvone Gebara speak for such a down to earth ecofeminism, proletarian, feminist and deeply ecological.

"I see that ecofeminism is born of daily life, of day-to-day sharing among people, of enduring together garbage in the streets, bad smells, absence of sewers and safe drinking water, poor nutrition and adequate health care. The ecofeminism I see is born of the lack of municipal garbage collection, of the multiplication of rats, cockroaches, and mosquitoes, and of the sores of children's skins.[5] "This sounds very much like an ecofeminist plea for the women in Somalia or the slums of Delhi and Mumbai, but not so relevant to those in Birmingham or New York city. Here ecofeminism becomes the semiotics of class distinctions in the liberation of women. The spirit of this discourse is similar to Christian Ecofeminism which combines spirituality with environmentalism and feminism.

"Christian ecofeminism is a fusion of the environmental movement, feminism and woman's spirituality"(Mary Grey)[6]. It is also a spirituality which "involves experiencing the world as sacred, held by sacred being, by God. God is not extraneous to the world, but the power of life, love sustaining and energizing this web of life." (Mary Grey, 487). It yokes itself with Liberation Theology which insists on Christian spirit and practice as the faith in God who "hears the cry and anguish of the poor"(Sally Mac Fague).[7] Christian ecofeminism views ecofeminism as reiterating this philosophical vision by contemporising it. Mercy, justice and caring are needed for nature which is suffering due to human cruelty and exploitation. At present, the categories of poverty are stretched: "...... nature is now the new poor." (Sally Macfague,quoted in Mary Grey, 488). The mission and ministry of Christian religion is 'ecofeminised' as "inclusive of the suffering birds and animals, of land turned to desert and streams polluted, and focused on the anguish of poor people sustaining life in these conditions" (Mary Grey, p.488).

Ecofeminism has had its resonances in India especially in the Chipko movement of 1973 in the Himalayan region of Uttarakhand pioneered by Sunderlal Bahuguna. It witnessed women standing unmoved around trees embracing them in order to resist the felling of trees and consequent deforestation by Government under the pretext of development projects.The Hindi word 'chipko' means 'to hug/ to cling'. Chipko movement was led by Gouridevi and 27 other women of the Reni Village. It was a non-violent social and ecological movement in

Gandhian mode by rural people, primarily women, to conserve trees and forests. Chipko andolan has had its off shoot as Appiko movement in the Uttara Kannada district in Karnataka state where 81 % of its geographical area had been covered by forest which shrank to 25 % by 1980. The local term in Kannada for hugging is 'appiko'. It was an uprising of the local people against the government's move to start industrial projects of paper mill, plywood factory, and a chain of hydroelectric dams for harnessing the rivers. In 1983 men, women and children of Salkani stood hugging the trees in Kalase forest to save the forest. Appiko andolan generated a new awareness of environmentalism in southern India and gave recognition to women as important role players in environment conservation.

Vandana Shiva the Indian scholar, activist and ecofeminist founded *Navdanya* – an organization for protecting biological and cultural diversity. She fought against the disharmony caused by maintaining the illusion that humans are separate from nature which she described as Ecoaparthied in her book *Ecofeminism* co-authored with the German ecofeminist Maria Miles.[8] She wrote about an eco feminism which is a unified vision of western and southern feminism accommodating under it environmental, technological and feminist issues. Vandana Shiva believes that the western practice of development serves only as 'maldevelopment' for third world countries, and calls for a restoration of a non - mechanical interaction between humans and environment which prevailed in pre-colonial India. Bina Agarwal, the Indian development economist and Professor at the University of Manchester in her essay "The Gender and Environment Debate: Lessons from India" addresses this issue and analyses the conceptual and practical aspects of ecofeminism in order to ascertain it relevance in India. She particularly focuses on rural/tribal India and its environmental issues with their class and gender dimensions. She offers an alternative transformative concept – 'Feminist Environmentalism'[9]– in place of ecofeminism. According to Agarwal's thesis, the participation of women in the Chipko Movement and similar acts of disadvantaged communities taking over environmental protection evidences the necessity for decentralized planning involving the rural poor, especially women in decision making relating to tree planting, scientific intervention in agriculture and sharing of indigenous resources. This is a radical environmentalism, a grassroots perspective focusing on the Indian socioeconomic context and considering the legacy of women's indigenous resources for production (especially in agriculture) and the history of bold and successful environmental protection that the rural women indulged in. Feminist Environmentalism is an Indian version of ecofeminism. It has its own conceptual discourse and dynamics of action in the approach to development. It addresses gender relations and relation between people and the non – human world. The outcome of this perspective is expected to be a degendering and declassing of the relationship between humans and nature whereby gender-power and production processes, and tradition and technology would support mutually, leading to an Indian development model appropriate universally. It involves a factual reckoning of production process, distribution of products, power and knowledge, and the formulation of development strategies from a grassroot level reality. Instead of rejecting technology and development, a studied and realistic approach to the *composition* of the products, the *technologies* used for production, the *processes* that led to the decision relating to technology and product, the *knowledge systems* on which choices are based and the class and gender *distribution* of products would facilitate a transformation in the relation between humans and nature (ecological dimension) and man and of women (feminist aspect) (Bina Agarwal, 151)

Ecofeminism may not provide lasting final solutions to women's issues or environmental concerns. Nature belongs to men and women. The concept and action of development cannot completely avoid expanding the resources of nature. Women's well-being and freedom cannot be confined exclusively to a condition of protected nature and environment. The independence and empowerment that technology has provided to women cannot be sustained by retreading to a machine free raw nature. So a balanced stance is imminent in ecofeminism. Alicia Puleo proposes a model called Critical Ecofeminism. It is the theory which avoids, with prudence, the dangers that the renouncing of development, the benefits of the rationality of modernity and the products of technology entail for women. Critical ecofeminism is an updated version of ecofeminism in tune with the new millennium challenges, simultaneously committed to fulfilling the promises of liberty, equality and solidarity of the enlightenment. It involves a clear awareness of the great levels of welfare as well as the destruction of the fabric of life that techno - scientific practices driven by modern rationality have brought about. Puleo's proposal does not reduce ecofeminism to a mere anthropocentric feminist environmentalism that safeguards and manages the national resources wisely. Critical ecofeminism insists on women's freedom to take decisions relating to their body. While rejecting the technological resources as elements of domination by capitalist patriarchy conventional ecofeminism implies a return to the image of woman defined by her role as mother and nurturer. Relating this role to her relationship with nature becomes inevitably retrogressive. "Conventional ecofeminism is an attempt to outline a new utopian horizon, addressing the environmental issue from the categories of patriarchy, andro-centrism, care, sexism and gender" (Puleo, 30)[10] The future of ecofeminism involves a clear stance in favour of women's access to free decision–making on reproduction which requires a significant role of women in demographic matters like the control and sustenance of population. This requires the support of scientific knowledge and technology. It is a philosophy which is neither technophobic not technomaniacal. The utilization of the innovations of science and technology should be examined in the light of Human Rights relating to health and healthy environment, the right to avail and sustain biodiversity, to avoid the sufferings of fellow beings and to leave the legacy of natural wealth to futures generations. Instead of positioning on the opposing side against man and technology, a sense of belonging to the multiple and multiform life of our planet, well informed about the uses and harm of technology is likely to charge ecofeminism with energy and ethics relevant to our times. No culture is perfect. Hence an intercultural understanding of sustainable cultures that give importance to human rights, and give special attention to women's rights and treatment of animals which ensures an internationalist vocation (Puleo, 32) is an integral part of critical ecofeminism. It calls for ecojustice and considerate understanding of the varied nature in the relationship between woman and nature across cultures and continents. The poor women of the so called south and the third world countries suffer more when the natural resources are taken away from their environment in the name of development or urbanization. The rural women in India depending on the nature for subsistence are forced to walk more miles for collecting fuel wood because of felling of the trees and deforestation, an instance of the 'rational' exploitation aimed at international market by which the rich urban women may get the benefit of techno economic development in terms of facilities that give her leisure, time and freedom from domestic stress. So a critical approach to gender stereotypes like the self – denying women who resist mechanization for safeguarding environment is necessary. For acquiring a culture of sustainability extremism of any ideology - feminism or environmentalism - is likely to be a hindrance. A wise balance needs to be struck between caring for nature and accepting developments modes facilitated by technology. It is a freedom that does not harm ecological well being. Critical ecofeminism necessitates a reconceptualization of the human being as one who "integrates reason and emotion." (Puleo, 33). Environmental education should include the precepts of critical ecofeminism and promote conviction about gender equality through ecology. A sense of fraternity comprising man, woman, and animals along with their habitat would fulfill the objectives of feminism as well as environmentalism. An ecological culture of 'Liberty, Equality, and Sustainability' is the objective of critical ecofeminism.

On examining the different perspectives on ecofeminism it is evident that a fully satisfactory concept that accomodates the women's issues and the environmental concerns in the contemporary globalised hi-tech world is yet to be established. Perhaps it is in the evolutionary stage. But it is true that the socio economic context in which women live is a crucial determinant in positioning woman in conjunction with nature ontologically as well as epistemologically. Defining ecofeminism in the Indian context is highly problematic due to the following factors:

1. The hugeness and the biological, the cultural and the geographical diversity of India.
2. The customs, beliefs, religious practices and daily life of Indians are inextricably linked to nature and our relationship with nature down the ages. It varies regionally across the country.
3. The ambition and planning for development, and making India a global player in economic matters is a significant part of Indian

politics and government at the central and state levels. There is a blind and unethical commitment (on their part) to development as a vote bank and financial resource.

4. Tradition, heredity, family orientation etc. have a great impact on the Indian woman's self which invariably block a complete avowal of feminism in spite of high educational qualification or high career status.
5. There are several 'divide's in India based on wealth, education, caste, class and even digital ability. Ecofeminism as concept and ideology has to tide over or accommodate these issues before getting acceptance in India.

Literary expression has always linked itself to nature in a symbolic manner down the ages. Ecofeminism has given a fresh energy and political dimension to women's literature. In fact all aspects of ecofeminism figure as theme in the creative writing of all languages and nationalities in diverse forms and combinations - from natural feminism which emphasizes the women's intuitive bonding with nature to aggressive criticism of technology and its disastrous impact on nature and a violent disavowal of the development discourse as alienating women from human rights and human emotions. Eco criticism includes ecofeminist vision and politics as significant characteristics. The interface of literature and ecofeminism provoides a plethora of inputs for the cultural and psychological understanding of this ever evolving concept. Ecofeminist literature is a magnificent epistemological mix - realistic yet highly imaginative, often sailing in fantasy - explorative, reverential to nature, dismissive to technology, feminist and futuristic. Ecofeminist literature has enriched not only the literary but also the conceptual resources of ecofeminism – a fascinating outcome of literature that genders the green and greens the gender.

## Notes

1. Rosemary Radford Ruether, "Ecofeminism: First and Third World Women", **American Journal of Theology and Philosophy**, January 1997, Vol.18, No.1, p.33
2. Bill Devall and George Sessions, **Deep Ecology: Living as if Nature Mattered**. (Salt Lake City: Peregrine Smith Books,1985) cited in Ruether, "Ecofeminism:First and Third World Women", p.33
3. Francis Bacon, **The Male Birth of Time : the Great Restoration of Man's Power over the Universe** cited in Benjamin Farington,**The Philosophy of Francis Bacon** (Chicago:The Chicago University Press, 1964)
4. Brownneyn James, "Is Ecofeminism Relevant?" **Agenda: Empowering Women for Gender Equity,** 1996, No. 29, p.9
5. Yvone Gebara, **Longing for Running Water** (Miinneapolis : Fortress, 1999) p.2.
6. Mary Grey, "Ecofeminism and Christian Theology" **The Furrow**,Sept 2000, vol. 51 No 9, p.487
7. Sally Macfague, **The Body of God** (London: SCM,1993) quoted in Mary Grey, "Ecofeminism and Christian Theology", p.488)

8 Vandana Shiva and Maria Miles, **Ecofeminism** (London:Zed Books, 1993)p.27.

9 Bina Agarwal, "The Gender and Environmental Debate: Lessons from India", **Feminist Studies** 18, no.1 (Spring 1992)p.151.

10 Alice H Puleo, "What is Ecofeminism?"p.30

# The Orizing Ecospirituality

**N. Prasantha Kumar**

Spirituality is a dynamic concept in contemporary socio-cultural context. In the contemporary sense, eco-spirituality evokes political connotations. It is part of the emancipatory politics evolved by ecofeminists like Carol J. Adams, Miriam Starhawk, Carol P. Christ, Judith Plaskow, Ursula King, Rosemary Ruether, Charlene Spretnak and Carolyn Merchant. Ecofeminists point to an analogy between oppression of women and degradation and exploitation of nature. They argue that patriarchy dominates and oppresses women on the one hand, and devalues and exploits nature on the other. Ecospirituality is an all-inclusive spirituality based on environmental conservation and ethics. Conventionally, spirituality is understood as part of an organized religion with a patriarchal and hierarchical structure. Spirituality has been institutionalized by political and religious hierarchy. Ursula King comments: "spirituality . . . has been cast in a dominantly patriarchal and hierarchical mode, where the spiritual quest was primarily the prerogative of a male intellectual, social and religious elite" (28). King means that spirituality was a privilege of the elite. Social institutions condition spirituality within the boundaries of tradition. But, personal accounts of spirituality from prophets or early Christian fathers or Buddhist monks or Rishis present spirituality through the image of a journey or an adventure into the unknown. It is regarded as a process of growth, transformation and enlightenment.

Maria Mies and Vandana Shiva argue that spirituality cannot be reduced to a monolithic definition. There are many perspectives and conventions related to the spirituality associated with ecofeminism. They identify two broad meanings of ecofeminist spirituality. Spirituality is an ambiguous term considered as an essential part of religion but not based on the patriarchal monotheistic religions of the West. Spirituality is a revival of a Goddess based religion. It is the abstract form of a manifest Goddess (17). The objective of ecospirituality is to regenerate wisdom required to liberate women and nature from patriarchal oppression and destruction. The notion of spirituality is therefore fluid, contingent and subjective. Mies and Shiva define spirituality as a "female principle, inhabiting and permeating all things . . . although the spirit was female, it was not apart from the material world" (17). This type of spirituality is constitutive of cultural and environmental issues. Karen J. Warren differentiates ecospirituality from other strands: "ecofeminist spiritualities differ on such fundamental issues as whether mainstream religious traditions can be reconceived or reinterpreted to provide environmentally responsible and non-sexist practices and theologies" (Adams 124). Ecofeminists consider the earth as sacred, as a manifest form of the Goddess or Gaia. They underline the interconnectedness and mutuality of all forms of life, immanence of divinity and a deep sense of community. The symbol of the Goddess conveys the spiritual power to challenge oppressive systems and to maintain life sustaining cultures. Amanda Porterfield explains the symbolic significance of the Goddess as a representation of "female powers of fertility and procreativity" and the female capacity for "insight and compassion" repressed in patriarchal cultures (236). The ecofeminists who celebrate the Goddess base their vision of society on the natural harmony between women and the earth.

Human civilizations and practices have been exploitative towards women, animals and nature. Women have been oppressed by the perception that they are inferior to men. Vandana Shiva traces the witch hunts of Europe as "a process of delegitimizing and destroying the expertise of European women" (21). Subordination of women has been well entrenched and continued through the exercise of coercive forces. The patriarchal domination of women denies them dignity, self-esteem and autonomy. Women have been confined to domestic captivity and denied holistic growth. They are subjected to cruel forms of exploitation and brutalization like prenatal sex selection and female foeticide, female genital mutilation, stalking, sexual harassment, control of reproductive rights and denial of economic independence. Historical and scientific principles have been appropriated to execute the devaluation of women and degradation of nature. Carolyn Merchant argues that the contemporary environmental dilemma can be traced to the formation of a worldview based on scientific reconceptualization of "reality as a machine rather than a living organism" (xvi). Merchant argues that the human domination over nature originated as a compulsive experiment for the "disclosure of nature's secrets" (188). She further contends that the new image of nature as a female to be controlled and dissected through experiment legitimated the exploitation of natural resources (189). Nature was objectified and feminized with a view to degrading and exploiting the resources. It is easy to equate nature with woman and then exploit or vandalize nature. Merchant traces this tendency to the mechanistic worldview based on the Christian myth of creation that perpetuates hierarchical dualism. Western thought has created binary oppositions where one term is privileged over the other. Val Plumwood defines dualism as "the process by which contrasting concepts . . . are formed by domination and subordination and constructed as oppositional and exclusive" (31). Plumwood explains dualisms as a system of ideas closely related to hierarchy. Social and cultural schism is reinforced through the creation of such dualisms.

Ecospirituality is based on personal experiences and insights of women. According to King, women's interest in spirituality is a means to "personal and social transformation, . . . a search for God and transcendence" (26). It reflects women's experience and quest. King argues that ecospirituality brings together the political and spiritual dimensions of contemporary life. The most important element of women's spirituality is liberation. Ecofeminists think that liberation accelerates social transformation leading to the creation of an egalitarian society. A strong kinship with nature and all forms of life expresses resistance to increasing violence on nature. Alice Walker cautions us against polluting the earth: "While the earth is poisoned, everything it supports is poisoned. While the earth is enslaved, none of us is free . . . . While it is treated like dirt, so are we" (*Living by the Word* 147). Ecological disasters from dangerous consumerist practices, rapid globalization, nuclear threats and heavy use of defoliants in war lead to unprecedented pollution of nature. Many activists find a connection between global ecological crisis and multiple instances of oppression of women throughout the globe. They want to liberate women and save nature by engaging and participating in anti-war and anti-nuclear protests and peace campaigns. Mies and Shiva explain the significance of protest: "Ecofeminism is about connectedness and wholeness of theory and practice . . . we see the devastation of the earth and her beings by the corporate warriors, and the threat of nuclear annihilation by the military warriors as feminist concerns" (14). Ecofeminists want to oppose the corporate control of natural resources and cultural destruction of societies. The ecofeminists combat various forces of exploitation. They wage protest for "environmental balance, heterarchical and matrifocal societies, the continuance of indigenous cultures, and economic values and programmes based on subsistence and sustainability" (Gaard and Murphy 2). The success of ecofeminism consists of organizing resistance and registering critiques of exploitation, of both women and nature.

Ecospirituality is a kind of alternate spirituality that resists organized religious practices. Scriptures have been interpreted from a skewed male perspective. Therefore, gender justice appears to be an elusive idealized condition in religious perspective. Ecofeminists attempt a subversive revision or reinterpretation of scriptures to establish a society based on equality and inclusiveness. They look forward to female divinity as a redeemer and a messiah. Ruether, the feminist theologian and revisionist Christologist, reinterprets *The Bible* and degenderizes the language used in the scripture to retrieve elements of eco-justice from Christian legacy (*Gaia and God* 141). Bart D. Ehrman argues that in the Kingdom of God proclaimed by Jesus, there would be no "injustice, suffering, or evil, in which all people, rich and poor, slave and free, men and women would be on equal footing" (179). This proclamation is accepted as a message for the underprivileged including women. Ecofeminists like Ruether envision a radical transformation of the patriarchal structure of society which is hostile to both women and nature. They see a grand alliance of all marginalized groups: the blacks, women, the working class, ethnic and sexual minorities.

Woman is constructed as the mortal Other based on the Biblical Theory of Genesis, the Fall of Man and his Eviction from Eden. Therefore, the negation of women is viewed as an attempt to retrieve man's immortality supposed to be lost in the Eden. Cultural Othering of identically-victimized groups is legitimated on the bipolar construction of the faithful and the heathen. The subjugation of the pagans and the heathens, and even their genocide have been justified as a way of maintaining the purity and power of God (*Gaia and God* 140). Ecofeminists like Ruether revise the scriptures to resurrect the liberating potential of Christianity at its beginning as a communion of the oppressed. Ecofeminists argue that spirituality is the same in all religions. Therefore, they raise their subversive voice not only against religious oppression of women but also against dogmatic faith and religious tyranny. They accept the plurality of ecofeminist perspectives and provide a cultural dialogue among ecofeminist subcultures. Ecofeminists argue that the notions of sin, penitence and salvation have been appropriated to consolidate the power of ecclesiastical hierarchy to exploit women and people of other faiths. This notion is extended to exploit the marginalized and the earth, and violate the basic principles of nature that sustain life. They resent the dominant androcentric bias in Biblical faith. Christ's critique of the Roman Empire, his vindication of the oppressed, his respect for women and his vision of the Kingdom of God promote complete and authentic humanity of women and similar marginalized groups.

Ecofeminist spirituality aims the reversing male hierarchy and promote women's communes and collectives as means to cultivate "an alternative culture of known hierarchical relationships" (*Sexism and God Talk* 194). The androcentric thinking pervasive in society and the church demonizes women as impure, polluted and sinful by associating maleness with the normative image of God. In this context, it is worthwhile to remember the infamous comment of Tertullian on women. He equated each woman as Eve and accused women as devil's gateway, as the betrayer of the Law of God, as the destroyer as the Image of God. He stated that though it was the woman who deserved death, it was the Son of God who had to die for her. The teacher of St. Thomas Aquinas, Albert, the Great, stated that "woman is a misbegotten man" (Barbara Walker 252). St. Augustine's misogynistic attitude is evident in his remark that "woman does not possess the image of God in herself, but only when taken together with the male who is her head" (*Women-Church* 138). She criticizes the universal devaluation of women and nature based on dualism endemic in Western culture. Val Plumwood argues that the logical structure of dualism has been appropriated to legitimate different forms of oppression: "reason in the western tradition has been constructed as the privilege domain of the master" (3). Nature has been represented as the feminine subordinate of the masculine master. as The identification of nature with woman is an attempt towards easy and unopposed degradation and exploitation of nature. According to Plumwood, women's equation with nature is a major tool in the oppression of both. This identification is a trap rather than a compliment (Plumwood 19). The nature-culture dualism is extended to the domain of gender and drives woman to an inferior position. Women's closeness to nature has been symbolized to construct the female subculture as polluting to the dominant male culture (*Sexism and God Talk* 62). Sherry B. Ortner argues that the domination of culture over nature is appropriated to emphasize the universal inferiority of women based on biological determinism (Rosaldo and Lamphere 71). Women's reproductive functions like menstruation, gestation, child birth, child rearing and so on are analogous to the natural process of biological creation and this analogy is manipulated to explain "the universal secondary status of women" (Ortner 83). Ortner maintains that this argument is a construct of culture rather than a fact related to natural process.

The misogyny of patriarchal society is perpetuated by the religious hierarchy as evident in the description of woman's body as the image of decay. Woman's body is often invoked with violent disgust as a contemptuous object that drags men to eternal damnation (*Sexism and God Talk* 69). The clerical misogyny legitimates the subordinate position of women in the church and the public sphere. The creation myth produce a hierarchical order where those at the lower level can be mistreated, desecrated, traded, sacrificed or slaughtered for those at the higher levels, including men and God. Thus, the practice of hierarchical dualism keep women and nature under the control of men. The estimate of terrestrial life as mortal, evil and the result of sin leads to a neglect of the earth and renewal of life (*Gaia and God* 139). Ecofeminists reject maleness as a universal principle and advocates full humanity of women: "Whatever denies, diminishes, or distorts the full humanity of women is appraised as not redemptive" (*Sexism and God Talk* 15). Ruether emphasizes women's autonomy and argues that the maleness of Jesus is not ultimate:

"It has a symbolic significance in the framework of societies of patriarchal privilege" (*Sexism and God Talk* 115). Assuming maleness to God is only an extension of idolatry that western religions despise. According to Ruether, "it is blasphemous to use the image and name of the Holy to justify patriarchal domination . . ." (*Sexism and God Talk* 19). As God alone is the father and the king, the message of Jesus means that human beings, irrespective of gender, are freed from the servitude of hierarchies of power. The hierarchical interpretation of messianism rejected by Christ was revived when Christianity became the religion of the Empire. Initially, Christianity revived and reinforced the subjugation and servitude of the marginalized and oppressed groups like the heathens and women. Christ addressed God as Abba, a compassionate and intimate father diametrically opposite to the image of a dominating patriarch. Ancient Jewish tradition imaged God as a female form, as a nurse or mother bird. Elizabeth Johnson argues that the naming of God as a patriarch is a hegemonic tool explored to "debilitate women's sense of dignity, power and self-esteem" (Russell 13). Ruether uses the term 'God/ess' to designate the divine, the "written symbol intended to combine both the masculine and feminine forms of the word for the divine" (*Sexism and God Talk* 38). She maintains that the term is not intended for worship, but a sign to capture the understanding of the divine. She argues that the term transcends patriarchal limitations of language and offers redemptive experience for all men and women. Ecofeminists call for more inclusive perspectives in the understanding of God and spirituality. The organized religions have realized the harm the traditions have caused to the environment. They have therefore evolved new ecologically sustaining spirituality and practices.

The western religious traditions have a strong connection to ecospirituality. St. Francis of Assisi drew Biblical resources like the tale of Noah's Ark and Jesus's Sermon on the Mount to support his ecospirituality and consolidation with the poor. In the Biblical tradition of kings, monarchy is not a despotic power but a source of benevolence. The gospels narrate stories of crowd sharing bread and fish in the wilderness. Thus, the Biblical tradition strongly endorses welfare of the community, sustainable ecology and protection of nature along with concern for the poor and women. Ruether finds the institutionalization of church as the reason for its misogyny and the disregard for the poor. She argues that women's wait for the church to reform itself is futile. Therefore, she advocates a twofold strategy: revision or the reinterpretation of the scripture and activist politics against the oppressive hierarchical structure of the church. Thus, revisionist theology is not simply a critique of male dominance in the church but of white, upper class male dominance (Miller 3). Marcus Garvey finds a growing discrepancy between teachings of Christ and the practice of Christianity (20). Walker also argues that teaching of Christ as an iconoclastic liberator have been misinterpreted to legitimate various types of domination and exploitation. After institutionalization, the church has silenced the voice of Christ and echoed the teachings of St. Paul: "Women are denied the attributes of speech, of self-articulation, of autonomous personhood" (*Conscience* 8). She means that the role and stature of women have been seriously undermined by the institutionalization of religious practices. Women's practice of covering the head while inside the church was said to be introduced by St. Paul to show women's subservience. Ruether disputes the maleness of the God and challenges the Christian contention that God is literally male. According to her, maleness is a metaphor for the rationality and power exercised by men in the public sphere. Since women were denied entry in the public sphere, God was identified with masculine qualities and came to be treated as a male (Loades 138-39). Feminine qualities of the first millennium were inappropriate to represent the characteristics of God. Women and the blacks underwent claustrophobic experiences in the church which denied them the sense of community, togetherness and righteousness.

As a prophetic religion, Christianity advocated revolutionary intervention of God to overthrow erring kings and rulers. This image has been appropriated as a tool of social domination in the organized church. Walker calls for a new epistemology of truth, knowledge and religion, and a new consciousness of the self in her treatise on womanism, *In Search of Our Mothers' Gardens*. Ruether calls for a change of perspective on female sexuality and women's reproductive rights in her article "Sex and the Body in the Catholic Tradition." Catholics and Protestants differ in their views on sexuality which she calls "puritan-prurient syndrome" (*Conscience* 25). In the puritan perspective, women's sexuality is viewed at the level of the super ego where sex is treated as a taboo but in the prurient perspective, covert female sexuality takes place in exploitative and violent ways. Briefly, women are treated as creatures beyond sexual feelings or as sexual objects to be used and abandoned. Therefore, Ruether exhorts women to exercise agency and control on their body, sexuality and reproductive rights. This enables them to free themselves from the sexual roles defined by patriarchy and church (*Conscience* 25-26). Ruether rejects the negative thinking and misunderstanding of women's sexuality and reproductive rights. She disapproves of this Christian doctrine which endorses procreative sex and despises sexual pleasure. She denounces the significance of sexuality as a relief of male concupiscence (*Conscience* 9). Ruether also finds Catholic aversion to contraception, abortion and sexual pleasure. Ruether also articulates her resentment towards unregulated reproduction which ultimately leads to the victimization of poor women, teenagers and people of underdeveloped nations. Therefore, she wants the church to endorse decriminalization of abortion, sexual education and contraception.

Ruether argues that sexuality is an expression of women's autonomy and self-realization. According to her, what is labelled as 'sin' is in fact a space of human freedom where "we have the possibility of enhancing life" (*Gaia and God* 141). According to her, sin lies in the "insistent perseverance in the resultant cycle of violence, the refusal to empathize with the victimized . . . and justify such unjust power" (*Gaia and God* 142). She challenges the notion of evil and tries to reinterpret it from an ecofeminist perspective.

The conventional view of evil as physical and social Otherness is a polemic view appropriated to punish the marginalized including women. The teaching that God loves you if you are good is unacceptable to her. She wants religion to accept life in its totality, to accept humans with all their flaws. Like Ruether, Walker also condemns church's control over women's body and exercising restriction on female sexuality. She criticizes the way religion has "systematically undermined and destroyed the sexual and spiritual beliefs of millions of indigenous people" (*The World Has Changed* 196). She resents the church's disapproval of homoerotic love. The ecofeminists emphasize fluid and autonomous body conditioned by spiritualized sexuality. They think of a society where women have sovereignty over their bodies and sexuality. Ecofeminists believe that sexuality can lead to higher states of spirituality. Therefore, they reject the religion's attempt to demonize and criminalize same sex love. They also encourage self-love as one of the possibilities of pursuing autonomy of body and sexuality.

bell hooks explain that women will not be liberated if they do not develop healthy self-esteem and self-love. She wants the feminist thinkers to develop "constructive strategies for change" in women's thinking about body and sexuality (31). Walker also states that women can achieve "spiritual growth and self-discovery . . . by paying close attention to their sexuality" (*The World Has Changed* 196). Walker points to the ecofeminist fascination with the human body as a resolute desire but not as a transgression of the Law of the God. Sexuality as an expression of malevolent desire is unacceptable to ecofeminists. Sexuality is a spiritual trope where women can engage in a constructive dialogue with one another to broaden spiritual enlightenment. Ecofeminist spirituality secularizes the term redemption and salvation to encompass solutions to social problems like racial and gender oppressions and ostracization of homoerotic love. They reconstruct the image of God as an all-inclusive divine figure beyond race, gender or class. God, to them, is a symbol of redemption or liberation for all human beings, irrespective of their ideological positions. Therefore, a consistent battle is fought in the racial politics of the West, challenging the institutionalization of religion and the legitimization of the racial imagery of the divine. Protection of the environment is a kind of self-discovery for women: an attempt to retrieve the glory and strength of their body, reinvent their sexuality and seek fulfilment in an elevated state where spirituality is inseparable from sexuality.

Judith Plaskow argues that spirituality and politics are not polar opposites. For her, politics is "an expression of spirituality in its intent to create more human institutions." She adds that "religion itself is transformed by politics" (71). In her perspective, spirituality is conditioned by contemporary realities. She insists that spirituality must be understood not in other worldly terms but as the fullness of relationships. Spirituality cannot be detached from our existence. It defines "ourselves, others, the earth and God" (Plaskow 71). Ecofeminist spirituality is a struggle to attain equality and justice as an integral part of spirituality. bell hooks also emphasizes the inevitable link between spirituality and political action:

> Feminist spirituality created a space for everyone to interrogate outmoded belief systems and created new paths. Representing God in diverse ways, restoring our respect for the sacred feminine, it has helped us find ways to affirm . . . the importance of spiritual life. Identifying liberation from any form of domination and oppression as essentially a spiritual quest returns us to a spirituality which unites spiritual practice with our struggle for justice and liberation. (109)

It aims at racial, gender and environmental justice for all. Ecospirituality incorporates images of female deity and native spiritual resources. hooks thinks that no transformation of culture is possible without a transformation of religious beliefs (106). Many feminist thinkers and writers have interrogated the sexuality of Christ. They consider masculinity of Christ as a providential choice rather than an accident.

Ecospirituality is a Goddess worshipping spirituality that shapes both women's spirituality and politics. According to Charlene Spretnak, women's spirituality is a revival of Goddess spirituality, an expression of personal and collective quest. It is an attempt to challenge the negation of the female in patriarchal culture (272). The term spirituality incorporates new connotations in feminist context: import, immediacy and intensity of feminine experiences. Gayle Graham Yates argues that feminists resent the use of the word religion for its institutionalized form. But spirituality connotes self-discovery and affirmation for individuals and groups (60). Women's spirituality suggests intuition, vitality and internal perception. Carol P. Christ argues that the symbol of the Goddess as the embodiment of spirituality acknowledges "the legitimacy of female power as a beneficent and independent power" (277). Miriam Starhawk argues that patriarchy has stifled the wholeness of womanhood and Goddess worshipping religions: "The Goddess tradition opened up new possibilities. Now my body, in all its femaleness . . . was sacred. The wild power of nature, the intense pleasure of sexual intimacy, took centre stage as paths to the sacred . . ." (14). She emphasizes the redemptive power of the Goddess. God is a metaphor that evokes the memories of a gynocentric past and the revival of a feminine principle in the repository of human experience.

Fertility is a prominent trope in Goddess based religion, which is also connected to the revolution of the moon. But it has nothing to do with sexuality. The mother image is a protector of young life, but all mother images cannot be generalized in terms of mother Goddess. The Goddess tradition validates the power of the female principle and shapes women's view of personhood and spiritual identity. The female centred spirituality is a rearticulation of feminine power in terms of pre-patriarchal imagery pervasive in ancient cultures. The Goddess based spirituality functions on the identification of sexuality and spirituality as complimentary to each other.

According to Starhawk, they are inseparable and inclusive: "Goddess religion identifies sexuality as the expression of the creative life force of the universe" (224). Audre Lorde also critiques the dichotomous relation between sexuality and spirituality. She speaks against the antithetical relation between the spiritual and the political. She argues that the spiritual and the erotic cannot be separated (56). Starhawk regards the Goddess image as a source of empowerment and a metaphor of a matriarchal society that existed in a remote past. Ecofeminism also believes in the natural process of creation as the source of ecological balance. The Goddess is co-creative with nature and human beings. Disasters in nature are consequences of men's contemptuous degradation of nature. The mother Goddess also symbolizes how ecospiritual rituals and insights can challenge patriarchal world view. Carol P. Christ states in "Why Women Need the Goddess?" that the symbol of Goddess is a "process of naming and reclaiming the female body and its cycles and processes". The symbol helps women to learn the value of youth, creativity and wisdom in themselves and other women. Carolyn Merchant argues that the witchcraft for the middle ages were different for men and women. While the witch was a symbol of disorder for men, it was a form of power for oppressed lower class women who fought against injustice and healed themselves through the regenerative powers of nature (155). According to Starhawk, "the three core principles of Goddess religions are immanence, interconnection and community... nature, culture and life in all their diversity are sacred" (22). Immanence means that spirituality is to be experienced here and now; we have to live our life with integrity and responsibility. Interconnection suggests that all beings are interrelated. Community points to the possibility of inter-special collectivity. In "The Laugh of the Medusa," Helene Cixous argues that patriarchy denigrates women's knowledge, insight and creativity as evil with a view to resisting women's autonomy. She explains how women have been culturally trained to fear the dark or black colour. Cixous makes a subversive reading of the Medusa myth to present an alternate reality. For her, Medusa represents the true inner self of a woman who transcends patriarchal control. In her view, Medusa defies patriarchal conditioning and enters the "Dark Continent" which is "neither dark nor unexplorable" (884). Cixous presents Medusa as not deadly but beautiful and laughing. Cixous calls upon women to laugh with Medusa to celebrate their liberation from the tyrannical hold of patriarchal culture.

## Works Cited


Christ, Carol P. *Rebirth of the Goddess: Finding Meaning in Feminist Spirituality*. Addison-Wesley, 1997.

- - -, "Why Women Need Goddess?" Goddessariadne.org

Christ, Carol P and Judith Plaskow, eds. *Womanspirit Rising: A Feminist Reader in Religion*. Harper San Francisco, 1992.

Cixous, Helene. "The Laugh of the Medusa," translated by Keith Cohen and Paula Cohen. *Signs,* Vol. 1, No. 4 (Summer 1976), pp. 875-93.

Gard, Greta and Patrick D. Murphy, editors. *Ecofeminist Literary Criticism: Theory, Interpretation, Pedagogy*. U of Illinois P, 1998.

Garvey, Amy Jacques, editor. "Philosophy and Opinions of Marcus Garvey." *Journal of Pan African Studies* (2009), pp. 1-63.

hooks, bell. *Feminism is for Everybody: Passionate Politics*. South End Press, 2000.

Johnson, Elizabeth A.. "Naming God She: The Theological Implications." In *Christian Ethics*, edited by Sandy Russell. 2000.

King, Ursula. "Women's Contribution to Contemporary Spirituality." *The Way Supplement*. Vol.84 (Autumn 1995), pp. 26-46.

Loades, Ann, ed. *Feminist Theology: A Reader*.John Knox Press, 1990.

Lorde, Audre. *Sister Outsider: Essays and Speeches by Audre Lorde*. The Crossing Press, 1984.

Merchant, Carolyn. *The Death of Nature: Women, Ecology and the Scientific Revolution*. Harper Collins, 1990.

Mies, Maria and Vandana Shiva. *Ecofeminism*. Rawat Publications, 2010.

Miller, Patti. "Rosermary Radford Reuther: Fearless Leader and Changemaker for Progressive Catholic Feminism." In *Conscience: A Commemorative Issue*, edited by David J. Nolan, Vol.31, No.3 (September 2010), pp. 2-4.

Ortner, Sherry B.. "Is Female to Male as Nature is to Culture?" In *Women, Culture, Society*, edited by M. Z. Rosaldo and L. Lamphere. Stanford UP, 1974, pp.68-87.

Plaskow, Judith. "Feminist Judaism and Repair of the World." In *Ecofeminism and the Sacred*, edited by Carol J. Adams. The Continuum, 1993, pp. 70-83.

Plumwood, Val. *Feminism and the Mastery of Nature*. Routledge, 1993.

Porterfield, Amanda. "Feminist Theology as a Revitalization Movement." *Sociological Analysis*, Vol.48, No.3 (Autumn 1987), pp. 234-244.

Ruether, Rosemary R. *Conscience: A Commemorative Issue*, edited by David J. Nolan, Vol.31, No.3 (September 2010), pp. 5-53.

- - -, *Gaia and God: An Ecofeminist Theology of Earth Healing*. Harper One, 1994.

. . ., "The Liberation of Christology from Patriarchy." *Feminist Theology A Reader*, edited by Ann Loades. John Knox Press, 1990, pp. 138-48.

- - -, *Sexism and God-Talk: Toward A Feminist Theology*. Beacon Press, 1983.

- - -, *Women-Church: Theology and Practice of Feminist Liturgical Communities*. Wipf and Stock, 2001.

Shiva, Vandana. *Staying Alive*. South End Press, 2010. Print.

Starhawk, Miriam. *The Spiral Dance*. Harper Collins, 1999.

- - -, "Witchcraft and Women's Culture." *Womanspirit Rising: A Feminist Reader in Religion*, edited by Carol P Christ and Judith Plaskow. Harper San Francisco, 1992, pp.262-68.

Walker, Alice. *Anything We Love can be Saved: A Writer's Activism.* The Ballantine Publishing, 1997.

- - -, *Living by the Word*. Harcourt Brace, 1988.

- - -, *The World Has Changed: Conversation with Alice Walker*, edited by Rudolph P. Byrd. The New Press, 2010.

Walker, Barbara. *Manmade God: A Collection of Essays*. Stellar House, 2010.

Warren, Karen J.. "A Feminist Philosophical Perspective on Ecofeminist Spiritualities." In *Ecofeminism and the Sacred,* edited by Carol J. Adams. The Continuum, 1993, pp.119-132.

Yates, Gayle Graham. "Spirituality and the American Feminist Experience." *Signs,* Vol. 9, No.1 (Autumn 1983), pp. 59-72.

# Environmental Awareness in Ancient India

C. Rajendran

Enviormental problems have been the focus of attention of the industrialised world ever since the publication of Rachel Curson's, *'The Silent Spring'* (1962), an epoch-making work, which documented the harmful impact of the use of DDT on soil and the living organisms. The earlier belief that the nature could be exploited without any sort of inhibition became thoroughly shattered by this and similar findings as man gradually came to realize the price he had to pay for the unbridled manipulation of nature. The enlightenment vision of man as posited against nature had to be given up in favour of holistic concept of the cosmos in which man also was a member. Nature no longer remained an inexhaustible resource to be exploited ruthlessly; her forests depleted and water polluted, the very existence of life on earth became problematic. Man became belatedly aware of the inbuilt safety mechanisms in nature like the green-house effect and the problems posed by phenomena like global warming, industrial pollution, depletion of forest wealth, the drying up of rivers and the like.

In short, man became more environment conscious. Against this background ancient cultures like that of India have a pivotal role to play in removing the slop-sided concept of development of the moderm man and in offering alternative visions of development and well-being. It has, indeed been widely acknowledged that it is the relentless vigil of traditional sects like the Vaishnoi group and Chipko Movement, drawing on traditional wisdom, which have prevented total deforestation in places like Rajasthan and Himachal Pradesh against the exploits of man's greed. If we delve deep into our traditional lore, the depth of the vision of our ancestors about our environment and the care they took to preserve it shall astound us. Here an attempt is made to explore the environemntal awareness reflected in Sanskrit literature.

Even in the Vedic era, which represents the dawn of human civilisation, we find a holistic concept of the universe of which man is only a part. The Rigvedic poetry shows the early Indian's intimate connection with nature. Most of the Vedic gods are personified forms of natural forces like sun, dawn, thunder, rain, wind and the like. But the most interesting concept in Vedic thought is related to ria, which signifies, apart from the moral order of the universe, its physical order as well, consisting of cyclic recurrence of day and night and other natural phenomena. The former somehow is regarded as the basis for the latter. The ecological significance of this is its conceptual similarity with the delicately poised order in nature recognised in modern science. Ancient Indians regarded the cosmos as an orderly whole, and considered trees and plants as infested with life.

Mahabharata explicitly states that trees have life since they grasp both pleasure and pain and grow if cut.[1]

An interesting hymn in Rigveda is about aranyani, the forest goddess (X. 97). The Rigvedic poet here describes the weird sights and sounds of the forest at night vividly. Plants are often evoked as divinities, along with waters, rivers, mountains, heaven and earth. One entire hymn in Rigvedic (X. 97) is devoted to medical plants (osadhi).[2] The vedic poets also refer to birds and animals, rivers and mountains, seasonal variations and other facets of nature. We see envirormental awareness, a much more sophisticated environmental awareness in Atharvaveda in Atharvaveda which gives a prominent place to herbal medicine and as such shows amazing awareness of the medicinal value of plants. Actually, Atharvaveda advocate a psycho-herbal mode of treatment in that it prefaces the administration of herbal medicine with the chanting of the appropriate mantra. The diseases mentioned include fever, leprosy, jaundice, dropsy, scrofula, cough, opthalmia, baldness, lack of vital power, fractures and wounds; the bite of snakes or injurious insects, and poison in general; mania and other ailments,[3] Macdonell describes Atharvaveda as the oldest literary monument of Indian medicine.[4]

The Ayurvedic system of herbal medicine, which developed in Indian soil, shows the intimate relation between man and nature in ancient India. Ayurveda belives that prevention is better than cure and the best way of prevention of ailments is living close to nature. Accordingly, great importance is given for ritucharya, the seasonal regulations by means of which we come to terms with the concerned season by way of appropriate food, excercise and lifestyle. Susruta maintains, in this connection, that kala or time, of which has the year as the body and the seasons as the limbs is a major point for consideration in treatment. Of all, six seasons are accepted by Indian authors, viz., Sisira (late winter), Vasanta (spring), Grisma (summer), Varsa (rain), Sarat (autuman) and Hermanta (early winter). The first three seasons are regarded as seasons belonging to uttarayana or the northern movement of the sun and human body is supposed to be weak due to this. On the other hand, during the next three seasons, when the sun undergoes the daksinayana phase, man is invigorated due to this seasonal movement. Picturesque descriptions are given in works like Vagbhata's *Astangahrdaya* about the various seasons and the change they bring about in the environment. Thus in hemanta, the sky and atmosphere (become) smoky, and the sun, less hot. With cold winds blowing, there will be a tingling sensation in teeth and horripilation in the body. Beautiful flowers like lodhra, priyangu, punnaga and lavali, surround the earth. Since digestion become strong, more sweet/saline/sour food is required. Since a person becomes hungrier in the morning, he should eat a heavy breakfast. Massaging and wrestling are suggested to keep the body fit. The same life-style is suggested for sisira, the late winter also.

In the spring season, which is portrayed very poetically, there is a sudden spurt of flowers and birds as well as bees become vociferous. The phlegmatic humour (kapha) gets aggravated in the body and produces nausea and indigestion. Strong inhalation therapy is prescribed to check this. Exercises and light food, consisting of old barley, wheat, honey as well as the meat of animals dwelling in arid forests are prescribed. Bathing and use of the pastes of karpora, chandana, aguru and kunkuma are some other prescriptions for the spring season.

In summer, since vayu gets accumulated, one is asked to avoid saline, pungent and sour things, as well as exercises and exposure to sun rays. Sweet food, which is light, uncluous, cold and liquid and diluted corn-flour, sugar, ghee, meat of wild animals, sali rice, milk, pastries etc, are prescribed. One should avoid alcohol, but can have cold buffalo milk. Walk in dark forests, sprinkling the curtains with cold/ fragrant water, and spreading flowers in the bed are some of other tips suggested to fight the heat.

In the rainy season, it is said that there is suppression of the power of digestion because of the heat coming from the earth and the sour change coming over water. One should use moderate diet, resort to fomentation, massage, and sleep in a place free from wind. In order to avoid vayu and kapha, one should use pungent, sour and alkaline things. Some of the dietary prescriptions include old barley, wheat, sali rice, meat of forest animals, garllic, old alcohol, curd, etc.

The autumn season (sarat) suddenly exposes one's body, accustomed to cold rain, to the heat of the sun. The pitta humour, accumulated in rain becomes dominant. One is advised to take bitter, sweet and astringent food. Water exposed to the sun durning the daytime and the cooling rays of the moon during night is to be used for bath. One should avoid exposure to dew, alkaline foods, curd, oil, animal fat, exposure to the sun, strong alcohol, sleep during daytime and the eastern wind.

Ayurvedic texts also refer to the perversion of the characteristic features of seasons due to vitiation of land and mention changes in colour, touch and smell in the environment due to various reasons. Mention is also made of the excess of flies, insects, mosquitoes and worms. Measures are also prescribed to cope with the epidemics caused by changes in the environment. Even if it may not be possible for us to find a scientific explanation for such prescriptions, the fact remains that ancient Indians were aware of many environmental problems as of today.

Environmental problems are addressed in works, like *Arthasastra* also, when dealing with settlement problems and the construction of new cities. Kautilya shows astounding ecological awareness when he maintains that sanctuaries (called abhayavanas) are to be set according to wild animals.[5] Private parties who come forward to set up a garden to orchard are to be encouraged by the state[6]. The land not used for agricultural purposes is set apart as grazing ground for domestic animals.[7] Kautilya refers to three types of forests, viz, those used for hunting (mrgaya) those for timber and other forest products and those for elephants.[8] There were provisions in the law to punish people hurting animals and the capital punishment was accorded to a person killing an elephant.[9] Fine is prescribed for cutting down trees and branches of trees.

Ecological aspects are taken into account in town planning also. Sanitation and water supply are given top priority by Kautilya. He recommends that some gap should be maintained between two houses. There should be provision to remove waste water from the buildings. If the drainage system is obstructed by somebody, it invites severe punishment.[10] Kautilya has also given astoundingly clear instruction for keeping the stables for horses and elephants clean with proper sanitary arrangements and separate fodder compartments so that food is not contaminated. Further, throwing up dirt and debris on the public road, contaminated public places with urination and disposal of corpses and carcasses of animals etc. are expressly prohibited.[11] Kautilya also refers to natural calamities like fire and flood, epidemics, famine and pets and environmental degradation brought about by them and suggests remedial measures also, whenever possible.

Ancient Indians gave utmost importance to environmental engineering when planning settlements or building new houses. According to Devipurana, the first thing to be done is the plantation of trees; then the building of the house should follow.[12] According to house construction manuals like Manusyalayacandrika, environmental considerations like the nature of the soil, its slopes, flora and the like are to be taken into account before one selects a site for residential construction.[13] The work also prescribes as to which plants are to be planted on different directions of the compound. Plantation of a tree is regarded as an auspicious deed and cutting down a tree is condemned as a sin. According to Matsyapurana, a lake is equal to ten walls, a tree is equal to ten lakes, a son is equal to ten lakes and a tree is equal to ten sons.[14] Such pronouncements bring forth the emotional bond that Indians had fostered with treees in particular and nature in general. If we go through the works of poets like Kalidasa, we can find that such gifted authors, apart from accurately documenting the rich biodiversity of the nature around us bring forth the emotional bond between man and nature, a bond which we have broken at our own risk.

## Reference


1. Mahabharata, santiparva, ch.184.
2. Macdonell, A. A. 1990. *"A History of Sanskrit Literature"*, London, p. 92
3. Ibid, p. 165
4. Ibid
5. Arthasastra, 2. 2
6. Ibid. 2.1
7. S. Shivaganesha Murthy, "Environmental Awareness of Kautilya" in V. N. Jha (Ed.) Envoronmental Awarenes as Reflected in Sanslrit Literature, University of Pune, Pune, p. 52.
8. Ganesh Prasad Panda, "The Attitude towards Environment Reflected in Kautilya's Arthasastra", V.N. Jha, op. cit., p. 47-8
9. Arthasastra II, 2. 9.
10. Sivaganesha Murthy, op.cit., p. 55.
11. Ibid.
12. J. G. keskar, "Land Zoning and Other Town Planning Principles in Ancient India vis-a-vis Environmental Awareness" in: V.N. Jha. op.cit., p. 217.
13. A. Achyuthan and Balagopal, T. S. Prabhu : An Engineering Commentary on Manushyalayacandrika, p. 17-22.
14. Sarngadharasamhita, Tarumanima, 5.

# Revisiting the Anthropocene in the Context of Green Literature

**K. C. Muraleedharan**

'Green Writings' obviously refers to a growing body of literary and non-literary texts that are mostly identified as giving prime importance to the sustenance of the unique planet, the Earth. One may come across various coinages to indicate such groupings of texts, like Environmental writings, Nature writings, and Ecological writings each of these deriving their validity from the particular contexts and disciplines of usage. 'Green writings' is preferred here for the relative freedom the word affords in referring to texts about the sustenance of the planet across disciplines. Green writings tell the tales of interaction between the human and nature or other forms of life on earth with the human species. The narrators being the human, it is the human account of animals and things in nature. So the human self-representation as well the representations of the nature often turn out to be highly problematic on account of its domineering politics. Another word that recurs in this paper in connection with green writings is 'anthropocene.' It indicates a contended geological epoch that is being debated and theorized. The officially accepted Holocene was said to have begun 11,700 years ago after the last major ice age. The debate in progress is whether we are in the Holocene or the Anthropocene. This situation prevails because scientific evidences of the human impact on earth captured in natural material like rock and ancient ice are required to accept the proposition of a new geological epoch. There are strong grounds on both sides to support their views. Anthropocene is not a formally and officially approved geological unit till now, but the debates in sciences, humanities and cultural studies point to a situation that it is impossible to ignore the proposition so casually. Interfaces generated through studies on the anthropocene in various fields of knowledge underscore its significance as a cultural construct in spite of the lack of proof adequate enough to satisfy disciplinary demands of Earth sciences. That the debates are presently not focused on the emergence as such but of the exact moment of the emergence also justifies the premises of this paper. Domineering tendencies have been visible at all times and climes and every discipline functions within the knowledge-power framework. In such a context, when the histories of all conquests are studied, it is necessary to revisit the trajectories of the anthropocene even as an imagined category, to make sense of the situation, as Simon L. Lewis and Mark A. Maslin observe, when a single species not just influences the present but dictates the future of the planet.

Etymologically speaking, 'anthropocene' as a word is derived from two roots in Greek language. 'Anthropo' means 'man' and 'cene' denotes 'new.'

The word stands for the epoch of the new man or human whose activities on a daily scale impacted earth and caused the extermination and extinction of some human and many other plant and animal species and turned out to be a threat to the existence of the planet. The term acquired currency and was popular only among a handful of geologists and climate scientists in the previous century when they ventured to differentiate the early human in terms of the intensity and proof of impact on the planet. Seth T. Reno makes a reference to the intervention of Paul Crutzen, an atmospheric chemist who won a Nobel Prize in 1995 for his study on the ozone layer, at an academic conference. Crutzen was said to have objected strongly to the use of 'Holocene' famously blurting out "Stop saying the Holocene! We're not in the Holocene anymore," reminding everyone there that, "we're in the Anthropocene". He pursued the debate further co-writing an article and contributing a follow-up essay in *Nature*, "The Geology of Mankind" (2002) and in effect starting the interdisciplinary field of Anthropocene studies. Crutzen's crucial intervention triggered debates spanning two decades. These debates going on since then have detailed the characteristics of the Anthropocene and suggested certain "big dates" like 1610, 1784, 1945, and 1964 as possible starting points. Paul Crutzen proposed 1784. As the debate proceeded intensely, claims for earlier and later points of time are also raised and some of these dates are 1610, 1945 and 1964.

Giving some attention to each of these dates or periods is necessary to move forward. The first date is 1610 and it is the first notable shift called the Orbis

(Latin word for the world) spike, the dip in carbon dioxide, viewed by the scientists as a significant cultural marker. Professors Simon Lewis and Mark Maslin designate 1610 as one of the potential dates of the anthropocene. The 120 years starting with 1492 when proto-colonial voyages commenced leading to the occupation of some non-European territories in the centuries that followed also becomes crucial in their consideration of the year 1610. They argue that the dip conclusively demonstrated that "humans are as earth changing as a meteor strike". The species swapping was unprecedentedly massive. It led to large-scale disruption of environment and death of fifty million people. It was actually a preface to large-scale colonization that happened in the succeeding centuries. Crutzen, as already mentioned, posts the inception of the anthropocene to 1784. For him, this year was a cultural marker, it being the year of James Watt's patent of the steam engine, a potential design that launched the Industrial Revolution and furthered the degradation of the sky, land and water bodies of the planet. Such developments even in the heartlands of industrial revolution in Europe benefitted only people of the ruling class and so some even consider the use of the word 'revolution' in this case a misnomer. The third proposed date in queue to claim the emergence of the anthropocene is 1945, the year notorious for the use of the atom bomb and nuclear tests having disastrous impact on the planet and its climate. The last one in the list is 1964 when the radioactive fallout reached its peak. Lewis and Maslin considered this year also as a potential start date of the anthropocene.

It may be noted that each of these four dates spanning over the five centuries are potentially probable dates for the start of the anthropocene. The first date 1610 suits the purpose of analysis here as it was the time of the emergence of the new human, the modern man, taking upon himself the task of creating a world centred on the enlightened man. The feudal world conceived and functioning with the god at the centre was being destabilized. The man wresting agency from god was emerging. Shakespeare's *Macbeth,* for instance, is a half-baked renaissance figure with a human will in action though the divine/fate is also present off the centre in the form of the three witches. By 1784, the new man of Europe goes a long way taking up the role of changing the world through scientific inventions and industries and establishing nations and colonies. The last two dates are 1945 and 1965. European supremacy faces stiff challenges from anti-colonial nationalisms in the post-1940s and by 1960s, the empire declines considerably.

A close study of the colonial ideology will reveal the identity of the dominant human of the anthropocene epoch as the ***white****, anglo-saxon, upperclass, heterosexual, able, normal, nurtured male* who controlled women, established colonies, exploited the working class and criminalized the other sexualities. This is true of both the European and the native upper class of the colonized societies who also practiced the othering strategies on the depressed classes, castes and women of their own or other communities. These four dates are significant in certain other ways too. For example, the 1780s is remarkable for the romantic discourses that substituted the neoclassical reason with emotion and imagination, and nature with culture thereby generating counter discourses to the dominant logic of early capitalism. The romantic anti-capitalism in their writings can be viewed as a cultural endeavour in redefining the human, highlighting emotional and imaginative perception of nature in the face of large scale degradation of the environment during industrial revolution. The romantic writers were earnestly trying to preserve in their literature what was being lost forever in the real world they loved and lived. Wordsworth brings into poetry characters drawn from country sides, sets his stories on the river and lakeside, and writes about peasants, the marginalized people, and women. The Romantic Movement is acutely political in the sense that it could generate counter discourses favouring nature and recording aesthetically the abuses and consequences of such degradations. So 1784 does not simply mark the start of the anthropocene, it definitely marks the rise of the self-critical stream within the anthropocene, one that attempts to redefine the human responsible to nature and other forms of life.

What is said above is true in the case of all movements that raised questions of rights and justice of those who are marginalized like the earth or nature. The black movements for rights and justice in America and Europe and African the anti-colonial freedom struggles challenged the concept of the dominant human - *the white, anglo-saxon, upperclass, heterosexual, able, normal, nurtured male*-and consequently the concept was redefined to include the black person when their rights were ensured constitutionally. In the same way, feminist movements have been taking up issues of male supremacy and patriarchy and fighting for their rights as human beings. In the context of their struggle the human has been redefined to include women. The working class was kept out of the definition of the human and rights denied to them. Like blacks and women, the proletariat were considered subhuman and made to work without rest. Movements based on the ideal of working class liberation asserted their identity and regulations to protect their rights were introduced, thereby reconstituting the human to include them also to a certain extent. The anthropocene transgresses the rights of the working class and it affects not simply those deprived humans but the environment too. So the human condition question is by itself a condition of nature question too. When the modes of organizing activities of labour, work and action was rethought, it was beneficial to environment too. The sexual minorities, the disabled and the mentally challenged are still in agitation like the organizations for human rights already mentioned to make the civil society accept their identities and render the human concept more inclusive. The point to note is that with the start of the anthropocene, the efforts to redefine it also began and the efforts are also going on to destabilize the global system that functions with the *the white, anglo-saxon, upperclass, heterosexual, able, normal, nurtured male* at the centre.

The dominant anthropocene is a figure alienated from nature, society and himself, and driven by capitalist and consumerist interests. In this sense, the new human is a male who controls and manipulates the earth (conceived as woman, Mother Nature). This inevitably places him in opposition to the non-human and nature. The logic of anthropocentrism defines the life of the dominant new human and green writings purport to destabilize the anthropocentric culture by infusing the non-human into the dominant concept of the human. The animal rights movement, the protocols for fighting climate change and regulations for conserving nature are also attempts at the redefinition of the dominant human to make it more inclusive and representative by accepting the identity of nature as a living entity with its own right to exist.

It would be proper to conclude the discussion on the anthropocene in the context of green writings considering a poem by the Barbadian poet Edward Kamau Braithwaite. The poem may show how the poet who is not a climate scientist or geologist by profession senses decades ago what the scientists have found about the anthropocene impact of 1610, in post-2000. It may amaze the reader to note that the poet conceives the landing of Colombus in the Caribbean islands as a toxic contact with the land which makes the earth and its creatures recoil and shudder at what was happening. He anticipates the knowledge of the climate scientists a few decades ago and articulates it poetically before such scientific writings become popular. roughly in the 2020s. A few decades earlier, this poem titled "Colombe" opens with Columbus watching the stars from his after-deck. In the morning, shadows lifting, beaches stretched before him cold and clear. Birds circled flapping flag and mizzen mast: birds were harshly hawking, without fear. Parrots screamed. Soon he was about to touch the land, a fulfillment of his long desire. Here the poet poses the question did Columbus vision the slaughter that his soldiers furthered there and observes that Columbus heard soft voices mocking in the leaves. He was splashing silence and the crabs snapped their claws and scattered in protest. These lines in summary speak of certain violations during the proto-colonial voyages and the violence committed on the peoples and land. But it can be seen that there is a greater emphasis on the responses of the non-human and the eco-sphere of the region which demands it to be reclassified as a green poem also though the earlier classifications prefer to identify it as postcolonial or anti-imperial poetic discourse.

What is suggested in the paragraph above is that the ways of looking at cultural productions and deciding their literary and political identity undergo certain radical changes giving prominence to ecology and concerns for the non-human. Even human concerns articulated came to be seen as part of the degradation of nature. It doesn't mean that the earlier classifications and the meanings generated from the poem lost their significance or turned invalid. A kind of re-conceptualization giving prominence to earth and nature has been underway for long in all fields of knowledge and it acquired the intensity of a green turn significantly when the marginalized began to assert their presence, rights and identity. With such assertions, these fields of knowledge have been reconstituted and what has been happening around the dates referred to above, namely 1610, 1784, 1945, and 1964 become crucial in the process of understanding how the anthropocene impacted the planet. Such assertions including that of nature leading to a deep green turn since the 1960s is a sign of the anthropocene interrogated with counter discourses. These probable dates of the start of the anthropocene thus turn out to be a context for revisiting its emergence and gather insights about the endeavour of green writings to refashion from within the anthropocene a human being that is at peace with the earth.

# The Ecological Turn in Contemporary Malayalam Poetry

E. V. Ramakrishnan

Questions of environment and ecology have acquired urgency in the wake of the debates on climate change and its impact on the future of human survival on this planet. Eco-criticism and eco-poetics have contributed towards greater sensitivity and critical awareness on the complex nature of the problem that cuts across many disciplines from Natural Sciences to Humanities. The term "ecology" is derived from the Greek word "oikos" which means home, household or hearth. At a deeper level, ecology is implicated in the way we relate to the world outside us and the values that inform those relations. There is a price to be paid for our rampant consumerism, and our inability to recognize that the resources of the world are finite and other living beings such as animals and plants have a legitimate claim on them. Anthropocene is a term that has gained currency over the last three decades, and it points an accusing finger to the human greed and ruthlessness. In discussing the ecological turn in Malayalam poetry, we will reflect on the manner in which human imagination has grappled with some of these issues.

By the late 1980s there were signs of shift in sensibility in Malayalam poetry. The modernist mode had lost its legitimacy as it was no more contemporaneous with the emergent social realities. Its highly charged imagistic expressions, in their grand sweeping movements towards the mythic and metaphysical, rendered the human experience remote and obscure. What was radical and revolutionary in an earlier context, began to appear insular and elitist. The best poems of Ayyappa Panicker, N.N. Kakkad and Kadammanitta Ramakrishnan, to name some of the most prominent modernists, had transformed the poetic idiom into something rich and strange. By early 1990s, one could see how their poetry had moved away from the resources of the local and the popular, as well as the political and the public. The shift from the high-modern to the post-modern had begun to appear even earlier, as the transitional poems such as "Samkramanam" (Metamorphosis, 1974) by Attoor Ravivarma and "Kochiyile Vrikshangal" (The Trees of Kochi, 1984) by K.G. Sankara Pillai illustrate. Both these poems point to the crisis of the high modernist mode. In Ravivarma's poem, an outcaste woman, condemned to lifelong destitution and humiliation is invoked in stark details, with no suggestion of redemption or salvation. In a subtle use of the metaphor of exorcism, the poet scatters her remains in the outer world, so that she merges into the elements. He wants her restless soul to enter the body of a man-eater "who descends on a village in the fury of hunger", her tongue becomes part of a wolf "that pounces on its prey when hungry" and her bottomless hunger burns with "the forest-fire/

feeding on cities and settlements" and her grief fuses "with the pus and blood of sunsets" (Ramakrishnan, 23). In these cosmic images, the wasted life of the woman returns to the universe to threaten its stability: "Let her curse become/ the scorching famine-striking sun;/ and let me drop her death/into the pock-marked sky/ like a burnt offering" (Ibid). Modernist poetry in Malayalam had not addressed issues of gender, caste or class. From that perspective, this poem marks a departure. However, in retrospect, we cannot but notice that there is a disjunction here between the abject condition of the life portrayed in the poem and its Sanskritized idiom.

K.G.Sankara Pillai's *Kochiyile Vrikshangal* is one of the early poems that confronts the ecological crisis emerging in Kerala. The poem laments the vanishing of an organic community in the wake of advancing consumerist culture. There was a time when the road between Thrikkakkara and Kochi was lined with trees on either side. The trees were transformed into commodities that were in demand all over the world:

Some of them became chants for Rama
Some figures of gods
Claws of demons
Racks for the condemned
Palanquins
Rafters and doors with fretwork
Some became lamp-posts
Some the fragrance of sandalwood
In Egypt or Greece. (Ramakrishnan,39).

The poem offers a critique of the predatory impulse of the capitalist society. In a land of vanishing trees, human values lose their relevance. The tragic lives of the poets mentioned in the poem, point to a climate of deepening alienation and isolation. The concluding lines of the poem describe how the toxic smoke of a disintegrating world chokes the possibility of human survival:

On a pyre lit by the raw firewood of excuses
Our life-long cremation.
In our eyes, nose, tongue
In our little obstinacies

Around the bag, the watch and the dream of the future

On the tiny feet long before the shoes –

the octopus-arms of smoke wind up for the crushing embrace
No, don't be in a hurry to get up!
Still there is enough time! (Ibid, 41)

KGS mocks the complacency and the lack of concern of contemporary Kerala society. Obviously, the mainstream was yet to be seized of the sense of urgency in matters of environmental crisis.

Women poets such as Geetha Hiranyan and Vijayalakshmi had taken note of the deepening gloom in the social world. Geetha Hiranyan's "Interior Decoration" shows her concern for the stunted lives around her. She speaks as a woman who stands witness to the patriarchal order of society:

But have no fear.
It will not spread out.
Roots will not cast their net
Into the depths of dreams
The tap root is clipped again and again
And again, by the knife of norms
Neither lust nor desire will
Erupt into the body's joy,
As the daily warnings
Regulate the branches.
(1991, 31)

In a world where women are not able to fulfil their potential, life's possibilities get diminished. This points to an erosion of values that sustain hope and well-being in society. Women become victims of development which sees nature as an object of possession and conquest. The inability to see the underlying relation between the human and the non-human at the root of our alienation. Vijayalakshmi's poem, "Martha" (1993) captures the anguished cry of the last passenger pigeon, Martha, which died in 1914 in the Cincinnati zoo:

Once we traversed the full sky
Like black clouds in large numbers.
We are extinct now, man unkind,
By your needs of bed and bread (Ramakrishnan, 58)

Man's greed and his search for unlimited comforts drive entire species to extinction.

Here, it is instructive to remember that Kerala witnessed one of the first mass movements for environmental conservation from the mid-1970s onwards. A massive hydro-electric project was to come up in the Silent Valley, one of the few surviving evergreen sub-tropical forests on the Western Ghats. Academics, writers and activists were in the forefront of the struggle to preserve the Silent Valley, mobilizing support across Kerala through their speeches, writings and public protests. The genre of ecological writing took off in Malayalam with this movement which succeeded in preventing the technocrats from having their way. The first surge of green poetry in Malayalam may be traced to this period. All major poets such as Ayyappa Paniker, Sugatha Kumari, O.N.V.Kurup, Kadammanitta Ramakrishnan, D.Vinayachandran, Satchidanandan, K.G.Sankara Pillai and Attoor Ravivarma contributed towards this tide of green writing that touched a deep chord in the readers' minds. This first generation of green poets, in their hymns to nature, spoke of environmental issues with great emotional charge and a deep sense of commitment to the public cause of conservation.

In retrospect, however, it is evident that the engagement of the poets of the 1980s and 1990s remained anthropocentric. Ecological poetry of the twenty first century has moved away from the liberal-humanist, individualist perspective that encapsulated the vision of the earlier generation. Contemporary poets show greater awareness of the 'the anthropological machine', to use a term coined by Georgio Agamben, which creates an absolute separation between the human and the non-human worlds, privileging the human above the animal and other organisms. That our planet is a live organism teeming with life of various kinds is often lost sight of. That life is sacred has been recognized in the abstract, but, in reality, human beings view nature as 'resources' meant for their use.

As we move into the twenty first century, the ecological awareness has deepened into a complex vision of many strands encompassing issues of socio-political divisions along the lines of race, caste, gender, religion, ethnicity and region; capitalist modes of development that have resulted in irreversible damages to the eco-system of the planet; epistemological models of analysis rooted in Enlightenment modernity that have reinforced an anthropocentric view of the world. The question of environmental consciousness cannot be discussed in isolation from the question of power relations in society. The 'greening' of Malayalam poetry is possible only when poets grasp the larger relation between the human and the non-human against the repressive regime of globalization and its neo-liberal policy frameworks. We need to recognize that 'the human' is produced by repressing the animality that is an essential aspect of the human. Hence the human remains an empty space with no fixed meaning.

Georgio Agamben, in his book, *The Open*, speaks of the human inability to relate to the non-human world on its terms without imposing man's perceptual and metaphysical world-views. The title of Agamben's book is derived from a poem by Rilke in one of his Duino Elegies (Agamben, 57). In the poem, Rilke speaks of the animal's ability to dwell in the open:

The creature gazes into openness with all
Its eyes. But our eyes are
As if reversed, surround it,

Everywhere, like barriers against its free passage.

Rilke suggests that we are constrained and confined by our humanness and unable to see beyond us. The human is always produced by an exclusion of the animal within man. The anthropological machine "functions by excluding as not (yet) human an already human being from itself, that is, by animalizing the human, by isolating the nonhuman within the human: *Homo-alalus*, or the ape-man" (Agamben, 37).

As we discuss some of the representative poets and poems of Malayalam from the last two decades in the context of the ecological turn in literature, our accent will be on the critical perspectives embodied in these poems. They consciously distance themselves from the hierarchies of order we have consecrated in our pursuits of modernity. 'Nature' does not figure in these poems as an object of adulation or worship. They recognize that we as humans are an essential part of the wilderness we celebrate as 'nature'. These poems are also about 'culture' as constructs that exclude and prohibit. They problematize the very act of writing poetry as in S. Joseph's "Letter to Malayalam Poetry" where the poet speaks as a rag-picker:

I live among the poor
In a thatched house like them,
I eat what comes my way
I have to bring water from far
Father calls me a dog
I have to clean up mother's shit and piss

I pick and sell tins, sandals, bottles, paper
People call me a rag-picker
Public buses do not stop for me.

He invites Malayalam poetry to his hut, where she would not trip and fall against household things:

You wanted freedom
Here it is in abundance
Can do and speak what you feel like
Can bathe in a stream
Can coo with common cuckoos
Sit on a mat on a veranda
Gaze at the sky
Owls will hoot, you will get scared
I will hold you tight with love. (2003, 10)

Canonical Malayalam poetry has been reluctant to admit experiences that do not privilege the middle-class view of art and society. Joseph breaches this invisible line by putting the everyday world of an outcaste at the centre of poetry. The speaking voice of the poem interrogates the consensus concerning the idea of the literary. For long, Malayalam poetry had lost its sense of the everyday world in the margins. When Malayalam poetry used folk modes of enunciation during its modernist phase, it was for aesthetic effect. The stark prose of Joseph's poem grapples with another order of experience which has never found expression in the poetic mode. By problematising the prevailing poetic mode, Joseph raises ethical issues related to self and expression, art and society, nature and culture.

In one of his finest poems titled "Basket", Joseph speaks of weaving a basket out of bamboo, palmyra fronds, stems of creepers and such materials we collect from village ponds shaded with thickets and rocks. As we plait the bamboos, it assumes the shape of a little sun. The manual work is accompanied by songs and endless chatter. Labour becomes an occasion for bonding between human beings. As the basket takes shape, it assumes many shapes and becomes a world in itself. Finally, it has to be sold in the market as a commodity in exchange for ordinary items for survival. The poet laments that baskets are no more made as in the past, as "palmyra fronds, bamboos and creepers have become scarce" and with that, "songs have ceased" (12). In his well-known poem, "My Sister's Bible" he shows how the real cannot be transcended through the ideal and the sublime. His sister's Bible contains mundane things like a ration card, loan application proforma, a notice from the merciless money-lender, a hundred rupee note and things like that, it has no preface, Old or New Testaments, maps or even the cover.

Joseph's poems move out into the open world of sunlight and physical activity. This is particularly noticeable in a poem he wrote in memory of Padeepan Pambirikkunnu, a Dalit writer who died in the prime of his life. The poem describes a journey into the interiors of a jungle, in search of forgotten scripts and numbers. In the images of the burning tree, bamboo groves simmering with fireflies, there are intimations of an intense affective aesthetics rooted in community experience. It is no more possible to separate issues of ecology from livelihood, community, everyday labour, breakdown of community bonds under the pressure of urbanization and globalization. In poets like Joseph, there is a deeper self-awareness of how we are being constituted by discourses of power. In the globalized post-modern world, we are caught in a web of images that dazzle and blind us. Poems create a counter-narrative to the spectacular and the sensational by highlighting the marginal and the minor. Ecological consciousness operates through a critique of the pervasive impulse of possession and consumption that is seen as legitimate and normative.

Veeran Kutty is another poet who deserves special mention in the context of the deepening ecological consciousness in Malayalam poetry. In a poem on the magician, he suggests that his magic is not all pervasive, it fails in crucial moments:

Please, anyone, can anyone of you,
Return this snake back into a stick,
It defies my command.
Please, anyone, will you stop me
From mutating into a worm or an eagle,
Against my wish (Veerankutty, 2013, 99-100)

The world is no more an enchanted place, and there is no way you can alter the real. It is in the act of reimagining the world that Veerankutty brings in a dimension of magic. He finds that nothing is stable or stationary in the world around him. Even the house which gives us a sense of stable belonging is only an idea which points to a void:

How do you say that the walls belong
To the room? It is the open

World outside where they belong.
If the walls do not belong to the room
The room does not exist
The house does not exist
My room and the house are in the world
Outside. Let me go home.
Don't call me back (2013, 125)

This awareness of the human as something not constrained within the domestic space and time, enables Veerankutty to go beyond conventional ideas of ecology. Everything in the world is connected, and the human is not an insular space. In "Embrace" he says: "The roots of trees embrace/ each other underground/ We had planted these trees apart/ fearing their leaves will touch each other" (153). In the poem, "On a Photograph" he speaks of a butterfly that comes to rest on a photograph of a war scene. Nobody remembers what the war was about or how many perished in battles. Had the butterfly intervened between the soldiers now lying dead, ticked them to break into a dance, they would have embraced each other. Before long, however, they would remember that they are 'duty-bound' to kill each other. By setting a butterfly on a war photograph, Veerankutty shows an alternative value system is always within reach. In such poems, there is a deeper awareness of the industrial military complex that shapes the directions of the present-day world.

Veerankutty's poems speak of transience and transcendence that reconstitute the world continuously. Our world contains multiple worlds. We fail to notice that there are several templates of time that inhabit our universe: the seasonal cycle, the time that a river takes to reach the sea or the seed takes to germinate, the time the light of the star takes to reach the earth. The "human time" is neither special nor unique. In one of his poems, he speaks of a yew tree in Scotland that flowered after a tiresome wait of three thousand years. One of its branches had turned female after such a long wait. He finds merit in obscene words as they help to cool tempers and articulate innermost thoughts. The sacred and the creative may embody their very opposite. In a poem which brings out the anxiety and anguish of the Covid epidemic, he speaks of a man confined to a bed in a hospital room, condemned to the same drab scene through the window. Then the branch of a tree comes into view as it moves in the wind, revealing a vision of reassurance and redemption. It takes so little to bring hope into a man on the brink.

The above discussion makes it clear that 'green poetry' as it is practised today, does not celebrate the human. Its focus is on the interactions between the human and other worlds. Hence, Agamben's idea of 'the open' makes sense as a frame of reference, to discuss the orientations in the new 'green' poetry. Our institutions and imaginations are rooted in the normative defined by the human as the limit beyond which nothing exists. The multiple worlds we inhabit have been rendered inaccessible by this obsession with the human. This semantic baggage is what is dismantled by 'green poetry' in Malayalam. In a perceptive comment, Agamben remarks that the forest is not the same to the hunter, the scientist, the way-farer, the nature-lover, the botanist, the carpenter, and the story-teller of fables (41). We tend to homogenize 'forest' into a set of 'meanings' which escapes its irreducible polyphony. We need a poetics of fragments, imperfection and fluidity to communicate the interconnectedness of the world. Poetry has to capture the plenitude of the non-human as a means of reclaiming our humanness. The mystery of living is never revealed through human language, but only through its cracks, breaks and silences.

It is the women poets that articulate this sense of interconnectedness of the world forcefully. In Savithri Rajeevan's poems, body is a presence that has to be confronted on its own terms. Old age brings frailty and dependence. "As you bathe your mother" is a poem of bonding between mother and daughter. The act of nursing the invalid mother becomes an act of reaching out after something vital within. In "Dehantharam", she mentions how the binary of the body/soul never allowed her to accept her body as primary and real:

Grandma maintained that
It was possible to exist
Without a body
Merely as a soul
Or ghost or illusion
Like the Yakshi atop the palmyra tree.

She never noticed her body till she recovered her eye-sight to view it from the outside:

Like India got a map,
I got a body.
The sailor taught me that there is
An ocean in the body

Rising waves, man-made ships, voyage
Across it, rainbow colors and skies
Reflect in it and conflicts and armours
Shimmer upon it
Yet which hitherto undiscovered
Continent is my body? This body?

The body is produced as a seat of carnal desires and physical passions against the idea of the spiritual which is grounded in the discourse of the metaphysical and the transhistorical. It is through such exclusions that we perpetuate a world of canonical meanings. Savithri's critique is directed against the masculine world order which is reproduced in the domains of culture and politics through exclusivist claims. Her poems attempt to recover continuities between the female body and its environment of attachments, entanglements and passions which were categorized as forbidden domains. In the 'othering' of the human there was the humanization of the animal. The 'anthropological machine' of the modern knowledge system, through its exclusions, produces a series of alienated figures such as the Afro-American slave, the barbarian, the Jew and the foreigner. By challenging the binaries which are at the root of all exclusivist discourses, the women poets clear a space of ethics where the non-human can be apprehended as an equal partner in the everyday world of exchanges.

In the poem, "The garden of nutmegs", Ashalatha revisits the myth of the fall of man in the garden of Eden. The grandmother in the poem questions the foundational myth of woman's subjugation. With a dismissive gesture, she rejects the threat of the snake in the garden: "All that was the rumours he floated". God is just a patriarch who sets impossible demands on the female. The garden with its lush green fruit trees and colourful fruits, does not appear to her a forbidden place of pleasure. However, her granddaughter, brought up on religious mythologies is hesitant and timid:

> She was unable to touch the fruits
> Which hung erotic, tempting.
> My hands stayed frozen
> Unable to raise a stone
> There stood a whole garden
> With the rich fragrance of temptation.
> (Ramakrishnan, *Anyonyam,* 162).

Grandmother who had violated the commands of God with no sense of guilt, was unable to understand her granddaughter's inability to cross the line set by patriarchy and its institutions. She reprimands her granddaughter:

> What kind of damned feminist are you?
>
> You can't even raise a hand to pluck a fruit! (Ibid)

A strong undercurrent of irony informs the poem. The female academics well grounded in the theories of Simone de Beauvoir and Judith Butler still find it hard to accept the body as the primary source of life and its spiritual yearnings.

One of the finest poems in contemporary Malayalam poetry dealing with the after-effects of globalization and its multinational hegemony in matters of human survival is "Thakazhi and the

Magical Horse" by K.G.S. The poem features the well-known Malayalam novelist Thakazhi Shivasankara Pillai whose fictional works are mostly set in Kuttanad, which is known for its paddy fields. He saw himself as a farmer and had strong bonds with the peasants in the area. In the poem, he is woken up by a nightmare: his paddy is being stolen by someone. He runs to the field with his companions, carrying torches and sticks. He finds the towering figure of Kandan Mooppan, the veteran peasant from Kuttanad known for his expertise in matters of agriculture, standing tall in the field. The poet calls Kandan Mooppan "the sage of farming". He tells Thakazhi that he had sensed something strange happening in the field and had come to investigate. And there it was, a magic horse grazing in the paddy, three persons tall, pristine white, with a fiery tongue. The horse was a 'one-animal army', a Trojan horse and out of it came an entire midnight battalion of horses. The field they grazed turn to barren in no time. Kandan Mooppan's peasants chased the magical horse away. Its tail continued to wave in the wind like the trail of smoke left by a bomber in its wake, blinding him. The paddy field now lay traumatised, violated, emitting the pungent smell of chemicals that corrupts everything in the vicinity: paddy, fish, crickets, grass-shoots, water-snakes, fog, water-plants and even words of truth. The poem ends with the lines:

> All that remains in sight is
> Pale bunches of grain, all chaff,
> Like bent backbones,
> With jingling hollow sound (KGS, 50)

The poem presents a dystopian vision of our possibility of survival. Kandan Mooppan is an archetypal peasant who knew the land like the palm of his own hand. He was not alienated from the world of the non-human and represented a social order where local knowledge and community bonds rooted in reciprocity shaped an agricultural way of life. With mechanization of agriculture and the introduction of fertilizers and genetically modified seeds, the world of agriculture became an extension of the capitalist world. Neo-liberal policies and the onslaught of corporate giants into the world of farming and seed production have cast a shadow over the entire agricultural community. The ecosystem of the paddy fields has lost their fertility for ever, and it stinks of chemicals. The proponents of new agricultural policy only think of increasing the farm output manifold. They fail to realize that the paddy field is a living organism where the water-snake, the fish, insects, plants and countless living things create a chain of living bonds between the elements of water, soil and air. When soil is polluted, the linkages break down and life cannot survive. The once fertile paddy field turns barren, breaking the chain of life that linked the human and the non-human. And that spells doom for the entire society.

## References

Agamben, Giorgio. *The Open: Man and Animal.* Stanford University Press, 2004.

Attoor Ravivarma, *Attoor Kavithakal* (The Poems of Attoor). D.C.Books, 2012.

Attoor Ravivarma, Ed. *Puthumozhivazhikal* (An anthology of new poetry). Current Books, 1999.

Joseph, S. *Meenkaran.* DC Books, 2003.

K.G.Sankara Pillai (K.G.S). *Trees of Kochi and Other Poems.* Sahitya Akademi, 2016.

K.G.S. *Thakazhiyum Manthrikakkuthirayum* (Thakazhi and the Magical Horse). Green Books, 2021.

Ramakrishnan, E.V., Ed. *The Tree of Tongues: An Anthology of Modern Indian Poetry.* IIAS, Shimla, 1999.

Ramakrishnan, E.V. *Anyonyam* (Quarterly in Malayalam), January 2021, Vol. 1, Issue No. 1.

Savithri Rajeevan. *Ammaye Kulippikkumpol* (While I bathe my mother). Mathrubhumi, 2014.

Veerankutty. *Veerankuttiyude Kavithakal* (The Poems of Veerankutty).

Veerankutty. *Iniyulla Divasangal.* (The Days Ahead). D.C.Books, 2021.

# Subaltern Presences : Women and Nature

**Anu T. Asokan**

"We are either going to have a future where women lead the way to make peace with the Earth or we are not going to have a human future at all." (Vandana Shiva, Lecture)

The common thread that runs through all of Mahasweta Devi's writings is the ethical vision of giving voice to the subalterns of the 'othered' India who do not find a place in the grand narratives of nation and modernity. In the process of interrogating the master binary, namely the dominant mainstream and the dispossessed subaltern, we also find that the binaries which authorise oppression related to gender, sexuality and class are simultaneously dismantled. Mahasweta Devi's narratives offer a scathing critique of the different kinds of oppression invoked in the name of development and progress. Her stories clearly bring out the nexus between ecological degradation and the exploitation of women, tribals and others from the lower ranks of society. Her works bring home to the reader the message that the liberation of women or any other oppressed subaltern group will not be successful unless there is an equal effort to liberate nature. Mahasweta Devi's women characters are subjected to multiple forms of victin hood and they range from witches, destitute, whores, wet nurses, goddess-like mother figures who are not conventional and homogenous figures having integrated gender identity. The construction of their femaleness arises from their unique situatedness in the environments they inhabit. The editors of *Women Writing in India* (1993) refer to this when they write: "Throughout Mahasweta Devi's varied fiction, women's subjugation is portrayed as linked to the oppression of caste and class. But in the best of her writing she quite brilliantly, and with resonance, explores the articulation of class, caste and gender in the specific situations she depicts" (235).

The marginalised or the subalterns in Mahasweta Devi's context include tribals, women and their environment. Devi's women characters mark their difference by expressing their resistance to their oppressors in both subtle and forceful ways. The women characters come from different class and caste backgrounds since Devi writes with equal passion about the rich and poor, the high caste and the low caste. This chapter employs an ecofeminist lens to analyse Devi's 'doubly displaced' subaltern women characters – whose daily engagement with nature is inextricably bound to a struggle for a living. I would like to provide a brief overview of Western ecofeminism in order to place Indian ecofeminism in perspective.

## An Overview of Western Ecofeminism

Francoise d'Eaubonne studied the connection between the dominance of men over women and mankind over nature and coined the term 'ecofeminism' in her work *Le Feminisme ou la Mort* or *Feminism or Death* in 1974. The ecofeminist movement is considered as a combination of the ideologies of both ecological and feminist movements. In the words of Ynestra King, "As the environmental movement along with environmental crises raised the consciousness of women to the decay of the earth, they began to see a parallel between the devaluation of earth and the devaluation of women. Women began to see the link as not a false construction of weakness, but as a strong unifying force that clarified the violation of women and the earth as part of the same drama of male control" (*Healing the Wounds* 106-121).The symbolic nexus between women and nature is attributed to qualities like care, nurture and biological productivity which have been essentialised with respect to both. According to Karen J. Warren, an eminent ecofeminist, ecological feminism or ecofeminism provides "a distinctive framework both for reconceiving feminism and for developing an environmental ethic which takes seriously connections between the domination of women and the domination of the nature" ("The Power and the Promise of Ecological Feminism" 124). Feminists as well as ecofeminists critique concepts like 'masculinity' which have been used synonymously with power, virility and superior reasoning power. According to Marti Kheel, masculinity is the sum total of the contribution of both good and bad characteristics which combines physical force, aggressiveness and male sexuality. Masculinity is equated with qualities such as rationality, universality and autonomy whereas femininity is associated with non-rationality, particularity, relation and dependence (*Nature Ethics* 2-3). Kheel acknowledges the concepts of ecofeminism set forth by her forerunners but she identifies ecofeminism as a philosophical representation which ties the concerns of women with the natural world.

Rosemary Radford Reuther, also a prominent ecofeminist, in her work *Womanguides: Readings Toward a Feminist Theology* (1985), examines the role of patriarchy in the subjugation of the natural world and women. She confirms that the constructed hierarchical roles in the society led to the domination of women and nature. One of the early voices of ecofeminism, Reuther studied the close connections between feminism, ecology and religion and came to the conclusion that patriarchal Christianity is responsible for domination over women and also for promulgating world views which led to ecological degradation. According to her "Christian tradition came to uphold a hierarchical dualism in which the male species was so named as the dominant lord" (62)

Critics like Anne Primavesi, Carol Christ, Carolyn Merchant and Charlene Spretnak study the role played by religions such as Judaism and Christianity and important civilizations to identify the perception filter that contributed to the subjugation of women. They hold responsible the creation myths of the major religions for initiating the humiliation of women and animals. According to archaeomythologist Marija Gimbutas, the earlier civilizations were more matriarchal and rarely militaristic but the invasion of the Indo-Aryans created a rupture finally culminating in the destruction of the pre-patriarchal societies. Gerda Lerner's studies focused on unfolding how the transition from the ancient Neolithic villages to the modern cities caused the evolution of patriarchal societies. The other factor which contributed to the domination of women and nature is the opposition existing between religion and science. Hostility existing between religion and science helped in the construction of hierarchical structures leading to the establishment of European and American supremacy.

Carolyn Merchant points out that the scientific revolution resulted due to a mechanistic approach towards nature thereby reducing it to the status of an object of abuse. She also refers to the Eden myth which has been reinvented to suit the needs of the mainstream narrative. She discusses how the myth is developed to provide a close relationship of human beings with the earth. She also notes how gender plays a pivotal role in the myth and critically evaluates human relationship with nature in the role of both oppressor and steward. In the introduction to her book *Reinventing Eden* (2003), she remarks:

Internalized by the Europeans and Americans alike since the seventeenth century, this story has propelled countless efforts by humans to recover Eden by turning wilderness into garden, "female" nature into civilised society, and indigenous folkways into modern culture. Science, technology, and capitalism have provided the tools, male agency the power and impetus. (2) Ynestra King, an American ecofeminist provides four basic beliefs of ecofeminist movement in her essay "Ecology as Feminism and Feminism as Ecology" (1989):

1) The first principle states that industrialisation subjugates nature and since women are considered closer to nature, the ecofeminists should engage and embrace all the struggles of nature, 2) The second principle critiques the human tendency of projecting a hierarchy onto the "interconnected web" of natural life in order to justify social domination, her second principle calls on ecofeminist theory to "show the connections between all forms of domination", 3) The third principle concerns diversity social and natural, which is necessary to the health and balance of earth's ecosystem. In order to maintain such richness of life, "we need a decentralized global movement that is founded on common interests yet celebrates diversity and opposes all forms of domination and violence" 4) The fourth and final tenet maintains that in order for humans to survive, we just need to arrive at a better understanding of nature of human and nonhuman and we must challenge the "nature-culture dualism." The result of this challenge will be a "radical restructuring of human society according to feminist and ecological principles". (18-28)

In the introduction to her work, *Feminism and the Mastery of Nature* (1993) Val Plumwood, prominent activist and ecofeminist highlights the four tectonic plates of liberation theory namely the oppressions of gender, race, class and nature. In her opinion, "Feminism has undergone major conflict, transformation and enrichment as a result of its encounter with other forms of domination and their theories, especially those of race and class" (1). Plumwood recognises the issue of treatment of nature which can be considered both in political and ethical terms. It is noticed that in the Western tradition, reason or rationality forms the basis on which mastery is determined. Historical developments have also played an important role in marking the various forms of oppression and there is always an association between the enactment of inclusion and exclusion of certain categories. The construction of masculine identity is not a simple definition. Plumwood states that it is a "multiple, complex cultural identity of the master formed in the context of class, race, species and gender domination" (*Feminism and the Mastery of Nature* 5).

The themes of racism, class and the nature of the Third World countries have been a point of discussion in ecofeminist discourse. Typically white women have been at the forefront in academia when it comes to voicing the concerns of women and nature. Laura Hobgood Oster observes that:

"Few women of colour have been able to remain in positions of leadership in activist or academic organizations for long periods of time. The political power of white women in these organizations undermines, often unintentionally, that of women of colour. Even though such organizations as 'Woman Earth' attempted to make racism as an integral part of the ecofeminist conversation, racial tensions contributed to the eventual disbanding of numerous ecofeminist dialogue groups. Even the designations "white" and "coloured" seem to maintain a binary within ecofeminism as it tries to subvert all such labels. ("Ecofeminism: Historic and International Evolution" 536)

To summarise, ecofeminism is a multi-stranded ideology that encompasses different theoretical underpinnings. In their significant work *Reweaving the World: The Emergence of Ecofeminism* (1978), Irene Diamond and Gloria Feman Orenstein identify three major visions – the spiritual, feminist and environmental.

The spiritual vision is rooted in the sacred envisioning of Gaia. Proponents of this vision look back to the golden age of the Magna Mater culture that flourished five thousand years ago in which women were equally valued with men thereby providing an example of an ideal partnership society. Communion with Goddess Gaia through rituals and worship, the forming of networks with other women and the forging of a new consciousness and a renewed covenant with the earth are the defining features of this vision.

The feminist vision is however distinct from the spiritual vision which accords equal value to all things in the world of nature. The feminist vision aims at achieving equal justice for all and tends to focus on problems of livelihood that women face and affirms action at the local level. In this vision the earth is valued not for its sacred nature but because it supports interconnected networks of people. This vision pays attention to the subalterns who are doubly oppressed by poverty, race, class and specially focuses on women in developing countries who are seen as the victims of patriarchy. The crux of this vision is the envisioning and praxis of a sound engagement with nature, which is intertwined with the needs of human beings.

The environmental vision shares the common vision of living in balance with nature with the other two strands. However its distinctness springs from its insistence for personal action affecting the quality of life as well as political action. Advocates of this vision espouse bioregional attitudes that help us fit better into nature by recycling and employing renewable resources. The envisaged end is an egalitarian society that is based on the equal participation of women and men which in turn fosters healthy ecosystems. This vision places the onus of nature stewardship equally on women as well as on men. A good example of this model is Wangari Mathaai who gained worldwide attention through her praxis-centred activism. Born in Kenya, a small country in Africa she started the Green Belt Movement, an initiative to plant saplings for regenerating Karaura Forest of Kenya, in the year 1977. The main aim of the movement was to provide support to the rural Kenyan womenfolk who had to endure hardships such the loss of water bodies, scarcity of food and firewood. Mathaai perceived the reasons of their disempowerment to be the causes such as deforestation, degradation and poverty. The women were provided training to plant saplings, conserve water and to protect the environment. The Moi regime and the dictatorship at the helm wanted to destroy the forest cover to cater the needs of the western countries. Her efforts to put an end to the regime proved successful and she was awarded the Nobel Peace Prize in 2004. These three visions are united in their critique of the devaluation and exploitation of women and nature by man and call for a realignment of values to forge a society based on equality and justice.

## Indian Ecofeminism: An Overview

India has some leading environmental theorists like Vandana Shiva, who is a biophysicist and social activist; her influential book *Staying Alive: Women, Ecology and Survival in India* (1988) hinges around topics like nature, culture, tribals and women. According to Shiva, the destruction of nature came into being with the construction of duality of culture and nature. She describes how the death of nature becomes a fundamental part of threat to our survival. Shiva condemns the progression in science which according to her is patriarchal. In the introduction to the book, she traces "the historical and conceptual roots of development as a project of gender ideology, and analyses how the particular economic assumptions of western patriarchy, aimed exclusively at profits, have subjugated the more humane assumptions of economics as the provision of sustenance, to make for a crisis of poverty rooted in ecological devastation"(xvi). The reductionist paradigm also views nature, women and tribals as insignificant in the production of goods and services. In her essay, "Development, Ecology and Women" (1988) Shiva articulates the position of Third World women, especially women of India. The instinct to survive prompts these women to have a closer affinity to Nature because of which she is known as "Prakriti", a life giving source. Shiva interprets the "death of the feminine principle" as "maldevelopment" forced on the Third World countries by the Western countries. She argues that:

Maldevelopment militates against equality in diversity, and superimposes the ideologically constructed category of western technological man as a uniform measure of the worth of classes, cultures and genders. Dominant modes of perception based on reductionism, duality and linearity are unable to cope with equality in diversity, with forms and activities that are significant and valid, even though different. The reductionist mind superimposes the roles and forms of power of western male-oriented concepts on women, all non-western peoples and even on nature, rendering all three 'deficient', and in need of 'development'. ("Development" 4)

In other words, progression in science and technology leads to injustice and marginalisation of women causing maldevelopment. Shiva asserts that maldevelopment tampers with the mutual co-operation among men and women and causes domination of men over women. She substantiates her argument by putting forth this argument:

I want to argue that what is currently called development is essentially maldevelopment, based on the introduction or accentuation of the domination of man over nature and women. In it, both are viewed as the 'other', the passive non-self. Activity, productivity, creativity which were associated with the feminine principle are expropriated as qualities of nature and women, and transformed into the exclusive qualities of man. Nature and women are turned into passive objects, to be used and exploited for the uncontrolled and uncontrollable desires of the alienated man. From being the creators and sustainers of life, nature and women are reduced to being 'resources' in the fragmented, anti-life model of maldevelopment. ("Development" 5)

Recently, developmentalism as propagated by the state has upset the dissemination of environmental activities in India. The uncertainties of the tribal leaders regarding developmental issues have often strained the discourse of environmentalism. The rules and regulations relating to the forests have always been stated on government papers and have never been enforced as a reality and this causes a problem. The essay by Amita Baviskar "Tribal Politics and Discourses of Indian Environmentalism" (2003) clearly analyses the class struggles between the middle class activists, tribal leaders and the tribal peasants in Madhya Pradesh. The enhancement of sustainable development forms the influential and emerging practices of environmentalism in India. Sustainable development promotes the viability of the needs of the present without hindering the ability of the future generations to meet their own demands. It also aims to bring about the unification of two important concerns namely, social justice and ecological conservation. The activists, both tribals and middle class, have common concerns regarding the environment, but the differences in their social hierarchy seem to affect their relationship. This calls for the serious attention of the writers while voicing the concerns that plague tribals.

Women engaged in a survival strategy in the rural parts and tribal areas find themselves on the periphery of the nation when nature and forest cover are destroyed. These issues cannot be resolved easily in the Third World countries due to multiple reasons. Privatization of ecological resources, ecological appropriation by state recognition of forest areas and commercialisation of forests are some of the reasons which have caused a disruption in the holistic understanding of the links between nature and the subaltern. Vandana Shiva remarks that:

> The World Bank social forestry projects in India were launched primarily to correct the one-dimensional commercial forestry that has made forest resources scarce for the poor; their aim was supposedly to enhance the availability of organic fertiliser, food, fodder and fuel for local populations. The result, however, is further erosion of their rights and resources. More than 90 per cent of tree planting under social forestry has been of eucalyptus, nearly all of it on fertile agricultural land, and all of it has been marketed to urban industrial centres especially to the pulp industry. (*Making Peace with the Earth* 118)

Bina Agarwal, Director at the Institute of Economic Growth, Delhi studies how women from poor households in India are victims of environmental destruction in quite gender-specific ways. In her essay "The Gender and Environment Debate: Lessons from India" (1997) she describes how the process of statization negatively affects the lives of women and the poor (96). She traces the history of statization starting from the colonial era to the present and discusses the various policies which were in force during the British period namely the enclosure of large tracts of land for timber cultivation, restriction of customary rights to the locals, scientific management of forest resources and the exploitation of forests by Indian and European contractors. Today, commercialisation allows the state a monopoly on forest resources and scientific forestry management measures set into motion by the British to further the objectives of profit and gain are still in vogue. Agarwal also distinguishes her view of feminist environmentalism as being different from the views endorsed by the likes of Vandana Shiva. Shiva, for instance, identifies the women of Third World as a common category of people who are exploited by various factors whereas Agarwal suggests that there are gender, class, caste and race-based differences in the division of labour and their responses to the various effects on environmental degradation. Agarwal asserts:

> Poor peasant and tribal women have been typically responsible for fetching fuel and fodder and in hill and tribal communities have also often been the main cultivators. They are thus likely to be affected adversely in quite specific ways by environmental degradation. At the same time, in the course of their everyday interactions with nature, they acquire a special knowledge of species varieties and the processes of natural regeneration. (This would include knowledge passed on to them by, for example, their mothers.) They could thus be seen as both victims of the destruction of nature and as repositories of knowledge about nature, in ways distinct from the men of their class. ("Gender" 126)

Yet another stalwart voice of democracy, environmental and social justice who raised anxieties about development, and the resultant displacement of people and its effects on the poor, tribals and women was Smitu Kothari. In his paper on "Whose Nation? The Displaced as the Victims of Development" (1996), he provides three contentions against the lack of incentive to incorporate the effort to reduce displacement and to introduce political resettlement using the wider socio-political context. The contentions are the following:

The first contention is that the current patterns of economic development which have been constantly invoked to justify the forced eviction of people all over the country, are themselves incompatible with the goals of creating wider conditions of equity and social security. The second contention is that the issue of displacement and resettlement has to be viewed within the broad question of distribution of power… The final contention is that political and ecological solutions must be sought which recognise the need to both democratise the control over the resources and processes of production, and regenerate the degraded ecological resources of the country. (Kothari 1476-77)

In 2001, C.K Janu, the tribal leader of Muthanga rebellion led the Adivasi Gotra Samiti, rebellion against the Kerala police's brutal attack on tribals who "occupied" lands and forests in Waynad. The agitation quickly gained momentum and the year 2003 saw the culmination of the tribal struggle and their ultimate repression by the government with the use of police force. This particular incident is highlighted as the "Muthanga incident" in the annals of Kerala history. Muthanga, situated in Waynad district, is a tribal area and constitutes mainly of the Adiya tribes.

The Adiya tribes belong to the strata of landless agricultural labourers and their area of settlement includes the Muthanga forest. The occupation of land by the government aimed at depriving their only means of dwelling and livelihood. The tribal agitation, demanding justice from the Kerala government was able to capture worldwide attention.

The rebellion by the tribals may seem insignificant to the "mainstream" discourses of power, but the role played by these minor tribes do emphasise the notion that they are the original inhabitants of the land. The majority of the tribal groups remain truthful to ancient beliefs of nature as a sacred presence. The message resonates with the "Reverence for Life" theory propounded by Albert Schweitzer in his work, *Civilization and Ethics* (1923) where he enunciates the truth that all life is sacred and each living being is inherently a valuable entity. The message highlights the necessity of a change in modern man's perception of tribals and nature as the 'Other'.

Mahasweta Devi writes about the indigenous tribes, women and nature of India highlighting the themes of extinction of tribals and disruption of the holistic understanding of their communion with nature. The modern world remains ignorant of the richness of the tribal culture and civilization. We can witness an anthropocentric pride as well as a hubristic denial of subaltern rights in the modern man who exploits nature without any thought of its repercussions. Tribal culture, which had hitherto been hidden from the gaze of civilization, becomes the centre of attraction in Devi's fiction. Devi incessantly asserts the view that tribals would like to lead a life undisturbed by the ruthlessly invasive modern civilisation and culture.

This chapter explores how ecofeminist concerns an ideology differs from their Western counterparts in a Third World country like India where both women and environment form the 'doubly oppressed'. It also examines ecofeminism in its varied perspectives by placing it as a study of caste, class, race and gender in a diverse country. The chapter seeks to explore nature as a subaltern category in tribal India through a study of the women characters of Mahasweta Devi's works who are closely identified with nature in essentialist terms. Devi's short story canvas in narratives like "The Hunt" (1995), "Five Women" and "Kunti and the Nishadin" (2005), "Draupadi" (1997), "Dhowli" (1990), "Bayen" (1986) and "Doulati the Bountiful" (1995) accommodates a wide spectrum of oppressed subjects ranging from women who vehemently retaliate at the unjust treatment meted out to them and their surrounding environment to helpless women who meekly succumb to the forces of oppression. Women are never given an inferior status in Devi's work and she untiringly documents collective as well as individual struggles by tribal women to establish their place in society. Devi's close association with women who partake in resisting against various oppressions such as bonded labour, rights to land, fight against dowry and other social evils influence her writing. In the essay, "Feminism in Mahasweta Devi's Selected Stories", Usha A observes: "The women characters are stronger when compared to men. The men appear to be lacking in insight into what is happening to their being, and remain, for a moment, passive spectators as their counterparts pass through the trying situations created equally by an indifferent establishment" (50).

The story, "The Hunt" tells the life story of Mary Oraon, a half-bred tribal. Raised in a small tribal village called Kuruda where residents lead "an impoverished and quiet existence", she remarkably plays out her social roles as a tribal even though pure bred tribals detest her for her mixed identity. "Oraons don't think of her as their blood and do not place harsh injunctions of their own society on her" ("The Hunt" 6). The Oraon community mainly depends on agriculture and according to Devi, they are the most advanced tribes in India because, "they took to agriculture long ago" (*Imaginary Maps* x). But Mary earns her living by selling fruits and other forest produce and therefore "She is accepted in the village society. The women are her friends, she is the best dancer at the feasts. But that doesn't mean she wants to live their life" ("The Hunt" 3). She has the freedom to pursue her beliefs. Mary is in love with Jalim, a Muslim which gives rise to a lot of criticism in her community. She subverts the socially constructed role of a marginalised tribal woman to voice her opinions intrepidly. She actively participates in the ritual of the hunt conducted during 'Jani Parab' once in twelve years where women indulge in gender reversal roles and assert themselves freely during this festival. The hunt is conducted to bring into play the spirit of community among women, "The women are all in the forest. Each woman has stood excited in front of her own door armed with machetes and the men's bows and arrows. As soon as the priest struck the gong they burst the sky with sharp hallos and ran forward" ("The Hunt" 14). Jani Parab or Jani Shikhar refers to the annual spring festival celebrated by tribals in the eastern India, especially in Bihar and Jharkhand. History also cites that it is celebrated in commemoration of the revolt against Muslims by tribal womenfolk who fought against the Muslims intruders attired like men. The process of the hunt is described as follows:

It is revealed that the ritual of the hunt that the tribes celebrate at the spring festival is for the woman to perform this year. For twelve years men run the hunt. Then comes the womens' turn. It's Jani Parab. Like the men they too go out with bow and arrow. They run in the forest and hill. They kill hedgehogs, rabbits, birds, whatever they can get. Then they picnic together, drink liquor, sing and return home at evening. They do exactly what men do. Once in twelve years. ("The Hunt" 12)

Hunting activity is traditionally associated with the assertion of masculinity. Moreover, it is an enactment of power play as hunting usually involves a struggle between the strong and the weak. The hunter being in power subdues the weaker prey and makes it surrender using the power of arms. The Oraon community gets to destabilize the established hierarchy of male supremacy once in twelve years. Karla Aarya observes that:

By performing the traditional male roles in a hunt, women demonstrate that the abilities related to hunting (sagacity, physical strength and knowledge about the prey) are not exclusively male-sex conditions. Those features can be also female qualities. In 'The Hunt', women can perform activities that are particularly considered manly .This is especially the case of the main character of the story; Mary. (53)

Mary Oraon upturns the conventional role given to the women of her community by involving herself in 'manly' activities such as taking care of Lachhman Prasad's bungalow, tending his sal and teak plantations, and his orchards and grazing his cattle. She is an independent woman who is aware of her rights as a forest dweller and she knows the government regulations that if there are mahua trees in anyone's land, the right of the fruits goes to the picker. Mahua cash crop is widely valued in the village of Kuruda because all the parts of the fruit are equally valuable, cooking oil can be made from the blackseed of the crop, the skin can be made to use soap and liquor can be extracted from the fruit. Mary guards the fruits of Mahua trees on Prasad's property and becomes aggressive if anyone tries to deprive her of her rights. Mary imagines herself as the leader, "she gets down at the train station like a queen. She sits in her own rightful place at the market. She gets smokes from the other marketers, drinks tea and chews betel leaf at their expense, but encourages no one" ("The Hunt" 3). Her super-efficiency coupled with her aggressiveness makes people fear her: "Everyone is afraid of Mary. Mary cleans house and pastures cattle with her inviolate constitution, her infinite energy and razor sharp mind....She stands and picks fruits and oversees picking, she weighs the stuff herself for the buyers" ("The Hunt" 5).

Mary also takes on the role of the protector of the interests of Prasadji, when her employer tries to get rid of the abundant sal trees in his bungalow when Tehsildar Singh, a contractor offers a huge price. Sal is considered as a sacred tree and is worshipped during the festival of Sarhul (during which the symbolic marriage of the sky and earth is performed), which is celebrated to mark the fertility of Mother Earth. But Prasadji considers these Sal trees as valueless and says, "Do you want to watch the flowers of a tree that bears no fruit? He wants to buy, we will sell" ("The Hunt" 7). The opening paragraph of the story signals the devastation caused to the sal trees in the logging industry, "It is a Sal growing area. Sal logs arrive night and day by truck. They are split in sawmills and sent in every direction" ("The Hunt" 2). However Mahasweta Devi astutely points out that the livelihoods of women are inextricably interwoven with the Sal lumbering industry. The contractor promises that women will be given eight *annas* for trimming branches and carrying the pieced timber to the trucks, additional incentives include a tiffin, a cornmeal in the afternoon, salt and cayenne with the meal. There is also the assurance that the honour of women will be kept intact. However the unscrupulous contractor wants to make maximum profit by denuding the Sal cultivated area and also makes sexual advances to Mary Oraon. The narrative of development is predicated on environmental depredation. He envisages a time when, "Countless trees will be ready for felling in few years... Soon these parts will be joined to Tohri at that end and Nirlaghat at this. Roads are under construction. Once there are roads, future transportation expenses will be saved" ("The Hunt" 8). Mary is quick to see his dishonourable intentions. She tells Prasadji, "That bastard tricked you. He took all the profit. Everyone from Tohri to Chhipador is laughing" ("The Hunt" 9). He undertakes the task of deforesting the forest and remarks with contempt, "Every five years or so some trees will be ready and I'll buy. One two three. This is still a *virgin area,* and I'll take the tree *felling monopoly*" ("The Hunt" 7). Tehsildar Singh represents the postcolonial symbol of power. Following the colonial rules of forestry he employs tribals of the area to deforest the Sal plantation and he offers them a pittance of tiffin and money in return for their hard work.

Like Mary, the Sal trees in Prasadji's bungalow are also hybrid. The usual sal trees found are dwarves in contrast to the tall ones planted by Mr Dixon. There is a strong connection underlying the planting of trees and birth of Mary. Mr Dixon sowed the seeds of hybrid variety of Sal and his son made Mary's mother pregnant. Mary is looked down upon for being of mixed origin but at the same time everyone readily accepts her presence in the society. Similarly, Prasadji complains about the Sal trees but he is later pleased to know about the amount it fetches on its felling. Hybridity which in general terms would mean the interchange of cultures but here the context forms a close association with the idea of Homi Bhabha's concept of hybridity. In his seminal work, *The Location of Culture* (1994) Bhabha views hybridity as the role of the powerful to assimilate the colonised under a unilateral framework but which finally ends in producing something parallel to the existing one. Bhabha debunks the notion of 'purity' regarding cultures since any culture is bound to bear the imprint of the preceding one that has occupied a position of privilege as the ruling culture.

In the story, "Draupadi" (1987), Devi presents a different view point of both nature and woman. As a Third World writer, Devi's primary concerns about the tribals and the Third World women especially tribal women overrides her other writerly nationalist concerns. According to Beniwal and Vandana, "Her stories are no propagandistic illustrations of ideology; rather the situation speaks for themselves, and as they evolve, ideology emanates from them as much as they themselves emanate from it" ("Writing the Subaltern at the Interface of Fiction and Ideology" 86). Devi's stories are iconoclastic and they often interpret myths in order to empower them to serve the tribal cause. "Draupadi" is one such example of her iconoclastic stories. Draupadi, the rebellious tribal leader, is subjected to the sheer brutality of the police. She is molested and gang raped by the police officials, but she asserts herself and her tribal identity unlike the mythical Draupadi. In the story, the character Dopdi "chooses to become the agent of her own deliverance. The Senanayak's perplexity and fear the end of the story is a classic example of the rupture of hegemonic discourse. Dopdi is the subaltern who speaks" (Rangarajan 92).

Draupadi, who is initially introduced in *Operation? – Bashai Tudu* as a young, carefree girl, fully asserts herself through rebellion and revolt in the story "Draupadi". She is *the* character who subverts the claim that subalterns cannot speak for themselves. She takes on the persona of a daring warrior of the Santal clan but is ultimately subdued by the army forces, committing atrocities under the guise of Anti-Naxalite Movement. She is raped and humiliated but this does not deter her from being an agent of reversal regarding gender roles. Senanayak, the chief army officer is forced to be silent under the transformed, fierce Draupadi who refuses to put on clothes as an act of protest against dominant males and tormentors.

A greater understanding of "Draupadi" can be arrived at by filling the gaps in tribal history. Devi rewrites a history which is dominated by the "mainstream" thereby filling in gaps and empty spaces with tribal history. She foregrounds the need to deconstruct elitist history which never gave importance to the original heroes of land. Devi's narrative fills in the gaps left in the national history thereby highlighting the rebellions and revolts of tribal communities against the "mainstream". Devi also re-represents her narrative pieces thereby portraying them as powerful representatives of certain historical junctures. Draupadi is a rebellious heroine of the Anti-Naxal period who assertively works towards protecting her community from the total erasure by the government and army. She is used as an agent by her comrades; she spies on the activities of the army and police and informs her fellow members. This shows the transformation and empowerment of Draupadi from a cloistered and protected tribal girl to a powerful rebel. Draupadi is made the leader of various operations of rebellion against the "mainstream". In order to prove their solidarity with the tribals, the Naxalites issue the proclamation that if Draupadi is reported missing they will to change their hideouts to pursue their struggle more vehemently, "They will understand Dopdi Mejhen has been countered. Then they'll run. Arijit's voice. If anyone is caught, the others must catch the timing and change their hideout. If Comrade Dopdi arrives late, we will not remain. There will be a sign of where we've gone. No comrade will let the others be destroyed for her own sake" ("Draupadi" 400). Dinithi Karunanayake comments, "The central character Draupadi or Dopdi, as she is often referred to in the text, is involved in a social movement—the Naxalite movement in India. While Dopdi is presented as a strong woman from the outset, it is at the very moment that she should become the "silenced victim" according to traditional schema that she instead emerges as an agent,"("Dismantling Theory" 4). She is respected by the Senanayak, the powerful dictator who proclaims to understand the tribal culture, society and their language.

Dopdi's blood was the pure, unadulterated black blood of Champabhumi. From Champa to Bakuli the rise and set of a million moons. Their blood could have been contaminated; Dopdi felt proud of her forefathers. They stood guard over their women's blood in black armor. Shomai and Budhna are halfbreeds. The fruits of the war. Contributions to Radhabhumi by the American soldiers stationed at Shiandanga. Otherwise, crow would eat crow's flesh before Santal would betray Santal. ("Draupadi" 399)

Draupadi is listed as the most wanted criminal in the list published by the police and army. They have been hiding from the police and Special Forces who were deployed to penetrate into the dense forest tellingly described as "dark" or hideous by those in power in contrast to the Santal world view in which the forest is the abode of nature deities and 'Jair-Era', the forest goddess. The forest belt of Jharkhani is a wild punishing space where the fugitives and Naxals who are ignorant of the forest topography are gunned down mercilessly in 'shoot-at-night' operations. Mahasweta Devi paints a vivid picture of the dynamics of the food chain that is triggered by their dismemberment. It is a typical Global South scenario which trickles down from the non-humans to the tribal lower caste humans. By the law of confrontation, their eyeballs, intestines, stomachs, hearts, genitals and so on become the food of fox, vulture, hyena, wildcat, ant and worm and the untouchables go off happily to sell their bare skeletons. Draupadi becomes the protector of these fugitives and is able to stall their killings in open combat because of her intimate knowledge of the forest.

Devi attributes survival skills to learning from the soil. The fugitives who manage to survive are those who have lived a long time, "In the primitive world of the forest" ("Draupadi" 396) they kept company with the poor harvest workers and tribals and these are people who learnt to let go of extrinsic book learning by rooting themselves in the knowledge of the terrain. This bioregional wisdom according to Mahasweta Devi will help survive against all odds. Both Draupadi and her husband Dulna who were well trained in guerrilla warfare comprehended the need to protect their oppressed community from the landlords. Surja Sahu, one of the oppressive landlords of the area rejected the fair share of their rights to paddy and seeds. He announces to the sharecroppers, "Increase cultivation with water. You want half the paddy for sharecropping. Everyone is happy with free paddy. Then give me paddy at home, give me money, I've learned my lesson trying to do you good" ("Draupadi" 398). He is harshly punished by Dulna and Draupadi assassinates him for his misdeeds. This induces fear in the local police about the magnitude of harm that can result to the "mainstream" community if the avenging duo were allowed to continue practising their strategies.

Draupadi and Dulna continue to be used by the Naxalites to track down oppressive landlords and hence lead a fugitive life in order to protect themselves from the police. Initially, a peasant group, the Naxals worked against the oppression of agricultural sharecroppers. The seeds of Naxal revolution were sown as early as 1966 by the Silguri group of Communist party where they initiated partisan warfare in Terai region. Their main aim was to fight against the "feudal remnants" present in the society and they later got the support of the tribals who were equally oppressed but by different forces of power. Considered as a major threat to the internal security of India, Naxals have long been able to mobilise the impoverished rural population and the landless tribal people. It should also be noted that these oppressed peasants and tribals were indoctrinated by the communist ideologies for many years. Spivak observes, "The target of these movements was long-established oppression of the landless peasantry and itinerant farm worker, sustained through an unofficial government-landlord collusion that too easily circumvented the law" ("Draupadi" 385). Dulna and Draupadi form allies with Naxals and in the story we can note that whenever there is retaliation against the "mainstream", the couple co-operated with them in the struggle against the oppressors. Moreover it can be noted that the forests became the site of skirmishes over the fight between the "mainstream" and the tribals. To the tribals, the topography of the densely wooded forest proves more advantageous than fighting in the open and in the story the couple Dulna and Draupadi concentrated their activities in and around *Jharkhani* belt. Dulna explains to Draupadi about the hardships of guerrilla warfare "Dear, this is the best! We don't get family and children this way. But who knows? Landowner and moneylender and policemen might one day be wiped out!" ("Draupadi" 399). The police of Banrajharh are on the lookout for the aggressive couple who fought against the "mainstream" and before being convicted for various crimes that have been taking place in the vicinity. They are described thus: "A black-skinned couple ululated like police sirens before the episode" ("Draupadi" 393).

Senanayak, the chief of army propounds the theory that it *"In order to destroy the enemy become one"* ("Draupadi" 394). He eventually becomes successful in killing Dulna, Draupadi's husband and staunch supporter of all struggles. Senanayak thought that his death would bring a fatal blow to the activities of Draupadi but she asserts herself in order to continue her struggles. It is to be noted that the government has been hunting Draupadi for trying to protect the oppressed. "Thus the search for Dopdi continues. In the forest belt of Jharkhani, the Operation continues-will continue. It is a carbuncle on the government's backside...They do not allow themselves to be captured in open combat in the next phase. Now it seems that they have found a trustworthy courier" ("Draupadi" 395).

Draupadi is however, captured in a final operation by the army. She refuses to reveal the hideouts of her fellow comrades and to divulge the facts of their various secret operations. Senanayak, tries to lure her using various tactics but he eventually leaves the camp providing instructions to his juniors that. "Make her. *Do the needful*" ("Draupadi" 401). The police rape and mutilate her body beyond recognition. The scene of rape is described as follows:

Shaming her, a tear trickles out of the corner of her eye. In the muddy moonlight she lowers her lightless eye, sees her breasts, and understands that, indeed, she's been made up right. Her breasts are bitten raw, the nipples torn. How many? Four-five-six-seven-then Draupadi had passed out. ("Draupadi" 401)

There is a difference in the representation of rape scene in the story. It is Draupadi herself, not a third person omniscient narrator, who recounts the events that she undergoes as a part of her interrogation. She acts passively when captured but she transforms herself after the brutal scene. She is no more ashamed to stand stark naked in front of Senanayak, rather the powerful Senanayak is silenced by the presence of naked tribal woman, "Draupadi pushes Senanayak with her two mangled breasts, and for the first time Senanayak is afraid to stand before an unarmed target, terribly afraid" ("Draupadi" 402).

In her avatar as an avenging goddess, Draupadi illustrates how women can never remain a mute spectator of the atrocities committed on land and community. According to the customs of Santal tribe, women were allowed to choose their partners and hence rape was not prevalent until the intrusion by mainstream. In the words of Anantha Sita Raman, "Santhals have also been cheated of their communal land by such dominant groups who entice the tribals to borrow beyond their means" ("Region" 15). It is significant that the Santali women who actively participated in the land alienation protests were those who were the victims of mass rape. The areas of forced displacement have always faced violence in various forms such as mass murders, gang rapes and other atrocities by the powerful such as the police and army. In the contemporary scenario ranging from the political rivalries to the displacement caused by neoliberal developments, like the Nandigram and Dantewada carnages have been unleashed on both women and nature. Judith Plant's statement regarding the link between the exploitation of women and the ecological crisis is of special relevance in this context:

> Ecofeminism is premised upon the social critique that the domination of women through patriarchy and the domination of nature through the Western model of development, are intrinsically linked. "The rape of the earth, in all its forms, becomes a metaphor of woman, in all its many guises." [1] Therefore the ecological crisis and the subjugation of women are two symptoms of the same illness. ("Toward a New World" 282)

"Dhowli" a short story by Mahasweta Devi depicts the dominance and silencing of a poor tribal woman and nature by the rich and the powerful. In contrast to the other two stories where nature provides a canopy and refuge, Nature is an indifferent spectator of the turbulent souls like Dhowli which is ironical since Dhowli depends on nature for consolation and livelihood. Dhowli lives at Tahad, which has a vast expanse of forest cover and tribals situated around the place depend on the forest for food, fuel and grazing of cattle. The forest appears like ex-situ conservation until spotted by road contractors and loggers.

In the view of "environmentalism of the poor" often also referred to as "popular environmentalism" or "environmental justice movement" (Alier 11), progress in technology and economic interests leads to vast displacement of resources and people. According to environmental justice groups tribals and the poor have been a part of nature or rather they have 'coevolved sustainably with nature' (*Environmentalism of the Poor* 11). We see a similar picture in the story, "Dhowli", where *Dusads* or indigenous communities mark forests as their homeland. Their rights to land are appropriated by the higher castes living in the village. The poor often become victims of subjugation since they are unable to repay the debt owed to them by the rich and gradually become the bonded labourers of the rich household. Dhowli's father borrows money from Hanuman Misra, a Brahmin and landlord of Tahad for her wedding. Her father dies and she too returns home after she becomes a widow and is wooed by Misrilal, the younger son of the Misra household who owns vast properties of land and a major number of bonded labourers. Privatization of both land and human resources has been a method of their exploitation. Kundan, the elder son of the household, firmly believes that since the poor are their slaves, they can be subjected to any act of injustice. He likens women of poor households to be similar to the plots ploughed and tilled by the rich. He ridicules Misrilal's love for Dhowli, "What a coward! No pride in his superiority as a Brahman. A man is not a man unless he behaves like one" ("Dhowli" 203). He asserts that poor and untouchables should be kept under their control. One can see the role play of culture over nature when Kundan reveals that he is incapable of handling the vast empire of nature, untouchables and women and expects his younger brother in taking forward the family lineage. He remarks "...It is too large an empire for Kundan to control all by himself- so much farm land and orchards, so many illegitimate children, so many fertile untouchable women, so huge a money lending business " ("Dhowli" 203).

Dhowli personifies nature as an empathetic protector and refuge in distress. This is evident when she invokes the thoughts such as "She was never afraid of the wolf or the hyena. They fear people just as people fear them. The forest felt so peaceful that the constant discomfort and fear she had after hearing the Misra boy speak so strangely to her was slowly going away. She was at peace again" ("Dhowli" 190). Dhowli finds nature a comforting companion and provides an image of lived experience, for she feels ecstasy in the lap of nature. She forgets the hierarchy prevalent in the society and all her sorrows of being a widow. The imagery of the forests is articulated in these words, "The forest in the early afternoon is primitive, gentle and comforting" ("Dhowli" 192). She envisages a utopian vision of nature which according to her would provide all the protection that she needs and also it extend the dream like pastoral refuge wherein she could forget all her distress, "In the solitude of the forest, the Misra boy was dauntless, telling her of his plans, and his words seemed to mingle with all the myths associated with the old forest, taking on an enchanting and dream like quality" ("Dhowli" 192).

Devi's narration foregrounds such grave social evils as prostitution and enforced rape that are codified and sanctioned by societal norms. It must be emphasized that in the case of rape by upper class there is an unspoken law that the tribal women who are raped are eligible for compensation. They are provided land for shelter and food for living. Dhowli is forced to become a *randi* or a prostitute because she was incapable of feeding her child a proper meal. She was not looked after by the Misra household and the society since she had fallen in love with Misrilal. The untouchables did not have the right to fall in love and to entice the rich. Dhowli retorts to Misrilal, "I spit on your love. If you had raped me, then I would have received a tenth of an acre as compensation. You are not a man" ("Dhowli" 199). Disowned by Misrilal, her body becomes a site of enticement for the contractors and coolies in Tahad. Beguiled by her beauty, the very same people start knocking at her doorsteps who have previously kept away from her for the fear of Misra household. The common threat underlying both Dhowli and nature is that they are perceived as commodities by the society. Nature is deforested for the economic needs of the rich on the one hand, while on the other hand, Dhowli becomes an object of sexual exploitation. Jennifer Wenzel observes that "The implications of Dhowli's story become larger, if not precisely epic, when the focus not only shifts from the forest to nature, but also to encompass a broader- perhaps even global-class conflict between "the Dhowli's" and "the Misra's," who now may even have nature on their side" (146). She also confirms that "Nature may no longer serve as the warrant for justice; its indifference however seems a product not of its autonomy but rather its subordination as the instrument of a greater injustice" ("Forest Fictions and Ecological Crises" 146). This needs to be substantiated with a reference to the closing paragraph of the story:

> Tears finally run from her eyes with the pain of this new injury. She never expected that the sky and the greens would be so impervious on the day of turning Dhowli into a public whore. Nothing in nature seems to be at all moved by the monstrosity of what is done to her. Has nature then accepted the disgracing of the Dhowli's as a matter of course? Has nature too gotten used to the Dhowli is being branded as whores and forced to leave home? Or is it that even the earth and the sky and the trees, the nature that was not made by the Misras, have now become their private property? ("Dhowli" 205)

Dhowli has always been a believer of pathetic fallacy a trope in which human behaviour is attributed to nature, and nature reciprocates by providing her all the necessities for her livelihood. It would be wrong to say that nature was indifferent to her feelings, for nature is also mutilated and destroyed in ways comparable to the sufferings undergone by Dhowli. Commoditized nature, in the short story can merely act as a passive spectator to the trauma of a simple village girl who has been forced to metamorphosis into a city whore.

Land and the subaltern woman are imbricated in dangerous ways as "Doulati the Bountiful" (1995), a novella set in the tribal district of Palamau demonstrates. This novella elaborates the bonded labour problem and the struggle for minimum wages for forest workers and agricultural workers which were carried out by Naxalites in Palamu (*Imaginary Maps* xix). In Doulati, Devi turns the spotlight on the exploitation of woman. In stark contrast to the tribal society where women are held in honour and the raping of the woman is considered the greatest crime, the hierarchical caste ridden land owning communities in places like Palamu regard women as mere commodities. Referring to how Doulati continues to be a living symbol for tribal and other 'untouchable' women all over India Devi comments, "For the flesh trade all you have to invest is two saris, a bit of food, some trinkets, and a bit of money for the parents. Poverty, poverty, poverty" (*Imaginary Maps* xx).

According to Gayatri Spivak, Doulati presents a servile truth which is the basis for women's subalternity. In the story, Doulati characteristics like sweetness, innocence, love for nature and responsibility put her in a vulnerable position. Spivak writes "Here woman's separation from organic intellectuality is a complicity with gendering cannot be perceived as sweetness, virtue, innocence, simplicity" (*Imaginary Maps* xxviii).

Doulati is compared with the feminine and life-giving earth which nourishes everyone. This maternal body is widely dismembered as if to highlight the fact that "Tribals are metaphorically and physically dismembered by this system" (Nubile 100). Syphilis-infected Doulati who dies coughing blood on the eve of Indian independence of the year 1975 over a map of India is a parable of postcolonial India (Jaidev 86). The novella traces fourteen years of gruelling labour and sexual exploitation that Doulati faces in the brothel run by high caste landowning Misras. Doulati is forced into brothel system since their father is unable to pay off a loan of three hundred rupees. Although Doulati earns over forty thousand rupees as a bonded slave in the brothel, the money is appropriated by the owner and she is left alone to die a painful death which is described in stark terms by Mahasweta Devi: "Filling the entire Indian peninsula from the oceans to the Himalayas, here the bonded labour spread eagled, kamiya whore Doulati Nagesia's tormented corpse, putrefied with venereal disease, having vomited up all the blood in its dessicated lungs" ("Doulati the Bountiful" 93). Although "Doulati the Bountiful" employs strategies of subversion to problematise the woman-nature connection the finer qualities like nurture and maternal care link Doulati's naturalness to the birds and bees and ploughed fields. In his essay on "'Doulati' as a National Allegory", Jaidev identifies *mamatva,* maternal, protected reward as one of the core motifs of the story. He draws attention to the point in the narrative where the female farm labourers break into a song about Bono the rebel who has fled from the bondage of the landlords:

In the wheat farm had landed
a pretty yellow bird
and inside, its beak is so red, so red! (96)

The song that they sing about the bird links this pastoral moment with thoughts of freedom. The children of these women labourers are compared again to little birds picking up wheat grains one at a time (*Imaginary Maps* 22). We find that characters like Bono and Doulati are capable of *mamatva* and this idyllic picture alleviates the gloom of the story and hints at the positive aspect of equating nature with women. However the larger metaphor drawn from agriculture is that of ploughing. Devi' writes:

> Doulati and Reoti and Somni
> Field work, digging soil, cutting wells is work
> This one doesn't do it, that one doesn't do it, the other one doen't do it
> The boss has turned them into land
> The boss plows and plows their land and raises the crop
> They are all Paramananda's kamiya (*Imaginary Maps* 59)

The image of the master turning *Nagesia* women into land and the image of ploughing the land serves as a grim euphemism for the carnal penetration of the woman's body which in its turn is a grim remainder of the dangers of essentialising women as nature.

Devi's narration also represents the effort on the writer's part to rewrite established epics to highlight the plight of indigenous communities who have been misrepresented or rather relegated to the periphery in the mainstream history. This can be called an act of remythicising. Ramon Panikkar, a famous theologian, in his work, *Myth, Faith and Hermeneutics* (1979) states "Demythicisation is necessary when one is unhappy with his 'myth' because the logos has already replaced it; but each demythicisation brings with it a remythicising. We destroy one myth- and rightly so if that myth no longer fulfils its purpose-but somehow a new myth always arises simultaneously"

(345). In "The Author in Conversation", the interview published as a preface to the book, *Imaginary Maps* (1995) Devi remarks ," The Ramayana, one of India's two ancient epics, seems to contain evidence of how they[tribals] were oppressed, evicted from their homeland, and then forced to occupy the lower reaches of the mainstream culture" (ix).

The collection of short stories from the book, *After Kurukshetra* (2005), revokes the powerful epic Mahabharata, since these stories emphasise a tribal reading of the great epic. They, however, do not detail the events and incidents of the 'Great War' and the lives of the royal families of both Kauravas and Pandavas. As a revisionary exercise, these stories, instead, voice the dissent of women in their various roles such as mothers, wives, daughters and lovers. The 'ordinary life' of the tribal women which demands high levels of endurance is referred to by Devi as 'janavritta', and is compared and contrasted with "rajavritta" the relatively easy lifestyle enjoyed by the high born women. In these short stories, Devi picks the powerful tribal women over the pampered women of the palace as strong indicators of ecofeminist values. "Five Women" is the story of five widows, who have lost their husbands in the war. These widows did not have the opportunity to identify the corpses of the husbands and mourn for them since all the foot soldiers who are killed on the war front are cremated *en masse.* These young women who are used to hard labour are hired in the royal court to become the companions of Uttara, the wife of the legendary Abhimanyu, who loses his life prematurely during the Mahabharata war. Uttara retreats into a shell after the death of her husband, because she is not able to summon the courage to interact with anybody. Her five widowed maid servants are named after five important life-giving rivers. By the way of introduction the eldest among them declares "I'm Godhumi. This is Gomati, holding my hand. That's Yamuna, with the red spot between her brows. That one standing there with a finger on her chin is Vitasta. And this is Vipasha, Vitasta's little sister" ("Five Women" 4). ' A closer look into their lives reveal that these women were farmers who had raised abundant yields of "golden wheat, jowar, oilseed, spinach, ginger, turmeric and sugarcane, so much more" ("Five Women" 9) Tilling the land and planting the seeds became their occupation after their husbands were forced to abandon agricultural practice and join the war since there was a shortage of foot soldiers. These men who returned from ordinary war did not do so after participating in the Great Kurukshetra battle. The royal family remained impervious to the grief of the common man but the earth which sustained them lamented their deaths in a unique way, "They say the pyres blazed for many days. That the earth was burning hot and baked rock hard" ("Five Women" 10). Uttara forgets the fact that prosperity which fills the royal court is brought about by these men and women who work in close unison with the land. Gomati, one of the five maids, is amazed by Uttara's innocence and her inability to hold an interconnected picture of prosperity as a network of toiling peasants working in close conjunction with the earth. She retorts, "You're really simple, aren't you? If the farmer's didn't pay with food grain, the royal granary would be empty" ("Five Women" 12). Godhumi bemoans the ravages of war which have brought about a serious change in cultivation patterns. She points out elegiacally that "But our fields, our rich fields, watered all year long by rivers, are lying bereft of crops" ("Five Women" 16). The five widowed women who are symbolic of the rape and mutilation of the land await rains to cool the parched earth. They plan to return to the village as soon as the earth retains its old fertility. They are acutely aware of their agency as stewards of nature and consider it their sacred duty to participate in the replenishment of nature's cycles. They reason with Uttara:

> If we don't go… the fields will lie fallow, the cattle will be uncared for. Once we return, all of us together will perform the necessary funerary rituals for our dead. The elders will arrange marriages. We need husbands, we need children. The village needs to hear the sound of chatter and laughter. We will…create life. That's what Nature teaches us. ("Five Women" 22)

The story ends on a positive note because these women look forward to a time when they can remarry, bear progeny and partake of the generative cycles of nature. Mahasweta Devi draws close connection between women and 'Prakriti', the life giving external world of nature. The story is a grim reminder that the desecration of 'Prakriti' would result in the negative metamorphosis of the life giving principle. Honouring the women therefore becomes essential for the well-being and fertility of the land which is in turn vital for the prosperity of the kings.

The analysis of the next story "Kunti and Nishadin" would be incomplete without positioning the history of forests in India. "Kunti and Nishadin" can be read as an allegory of the accelerating deforestation in India with majority of the forest being cut down for developmental needs.

"Kunti and Nishadin", recounts the story of Kunti, the mother of Pandavas who has retreated into an ashram, in the Dhankaranya forest in order to spend the last days of her life. Kunti is overwhelmed by grief by the heavy death toll and loss of lives on both sides in the Holy War and carries within herself a "burden of unspoken thoughts and feelings" ("Kunti and Nishadin" 26). Recollecting the massive carnage and the death toll, she recalls, "O Devi Vasundhara! O Mother Earth! After Kurukshetra, countless funeral pyres were lit. All those foot soldiers who were drafted from faraway lands and who sacrificed their lives in the battle, were at Yudhisthira's orders, organised on mass pyres organised by Vidura" ("Kunti and Nishadin" 32). She observes how the *nishadins* lead a carefree life on account of the oneness of feeling they share with the forest whereas she is unable to speak her thoughts since her mind is cluttered and ill at ease. Kunti recalls the insightful words of Vidura, half-brother of Pandu and minister at their court, "Kunti", He has said, Aranyaka, the spirit of the forest, herself shies away from human beings. She knows the forest tribes well. They never lose their way. But Aranyaka's magic leads the outsiders astray" ("Kunti and Nishadin" 31). As a backdrop, to this main story we have a narrative about the feelings of revenge and fury in the minds of tribals - these original forest dwellers, about the burning of the Khandava forest which is glossed over in the mainstream epic as the need to feed the consumptive hunger of Agni, the God of Fire. Philip Lutgendorf interprets, "But Agni doesn't simply desire wood and land: he wants "the fat of the living," and so Krsna and his friend cheerfully use their warrior prowess to seal off the perimeters of the forest, conduct a "vast massacre" of its fleeing creatures, and hurl their bodies into flames" ("City, Forest, and Cosmos" 275). Kunti carries the burden of guilt, she mourns the death of Gandhari's sons and deeply repents the act of concealing the truth about her first born illegitimate son, Karna. Kunti lapses into recall and reverie while taking her routine walk through the forest and by exteriorising her thoughts, she thinks, "Today Kunti would ask mother Earth, where had she gone wrong, what was her crime, when would she be able to forgive herself?" ("Kunti and Nishadin" 35). She feels that she should divest herself of moral obligations, "If only she could unburden herself to this forest, these rocks, birds, insects, withered leaves!" ("Kunti and Nishadin" 26). The forest gradually assumes the role of the teacher and Kunti realises that "Thus this lonely forest, this closeness to nature, the daily sunsets-all this shows me how petty and ignoble human beings are"(Kunti and Nishadin 29). The *nishadins* observe Kunti from afar and an elderly *nishadin* approaches Kunti and even tries to talk to her but she fears of their proximity as their language is totally incomprehensible to her. She pleads to nature to listen to her troubles,

"O Mother Earth, protector of the forests-hills-waters and all living things, hear what Kunti has to say! ... I was overwhelmed to find my sons alive after the battle of Kurukshetra. But Draupadi and Uttara were devastated at the death of their sons.... The chapter of death is now past. Come, let us dry our tears. We must not allow ourselves to be undone by grief. Harden your hearts. Of course death is nothing but an epic of sorrow. But we wives, mothers, daughters, sisters have to live on. To survive we need courage and the strength to bear pain. Because this grief is going to be our life long companions. ("Kunti and Nishadin" 29)

Her confession is interrupted by the elderly *nishadin* who approaches her saying that the tribal community in the forest have been waiting for years to talk to her. Kunti is astonished to learn that the *janavritta* can speak her language when the elderly *nishadin* comments "Oh yes, I not only understand it, I speak it too. Of course you never thought of us as human, did you? No more than the mute rocks, or trees, or animals" ("Kunti and Nishadin" 35). The elderly *Nishadin* goes on to accuse Kunti of burning the lac palace thereby causing the death of six innocent people from the *Nishadin* tribe. In order to thwart the plan of *Kauravas,* Kunti disguises six tribals as herself and her five sons. Although the plan is successful and saves the *Pandavas* the gory deaths of the six *nishadins* who are scapegoated in the lac palace are banished from public memory. Elderly *nishadin* reminds her: "You couldn't even remember this sin. Causing six innocent forest tribals to be burnt to death to serve your own interests. That was not even a crime in your book. In our eyes, by the laws of Mother Nature, you, your sons, your allies are all held guilty ("Kunti and Nishadin" 38).

The elderly *nishadin* curses Kunti and clarifies "To beg forgiveness is typical of the rajavritta. We don't understand such things. When the five of us came away here, others came with us. For years, this forest has looked after us" ("Kunti and Nishadin" 39). Highlighting the renewing capability of the earth the *nishadin* comments, "The fire will do its work, then rain will quench the flames. The scorched earth will turn green again" ("Kunti and Nishadin 39).The *nishadins* have sensed the outbreak of a forest fire and hence they are fleeing from the place. Kunti, guilty of her worldly crimes waits for death even in the mouth of engulfing flames. She ruminates "Burning alive in the flames of a forest fire, will she pray for forgiveness from a certain dear nishadin? In the rajavritta does one beg forgiveness for killing the innocent?" ("Kunti and Nishadin" 39).

The play "Bayen" draws our attention to the practice of witch hunt in India, found in the belts of dense tribal population where women are mainly accused or branded witches for various reasons. Chandidasi, the primary character of the play is declared a *bayen* by the society due to ominous deaths recurring in the community. The story mirrors and critiques the social construction of women as witches which continue to be prevalent in the present day society. Ranjana Kumari, President of Centre for Social Research (Delhi) comments,

"India has a patriarchal society and women here are tortured in the name of many myths and taboos. Crimes relating to witch-hunting are basically committed against the women by family members along with the village authorities and so, the State's responsibility towards the victim is highly necessary but unfortunately the rising torture trend show that the government has actually failed to act against this heinous crime." *(Zee News 2012)*

Chandidasi, belongs to the Dome community whose male members take on the task of burying the dead. In order to arrive at a deeper understanding of the Dome community and their vocation one must look back into the history of Scheduled Tribes in India. The etymology of the tribe name, 'Dome' can be traced to the Sanskrit word 'damaru'- the drum which indicates that the members of the community were hunter-gatherers before being enlisted as scheduled tribe. Their main vocation includes scavenging, burying the dead and basket weaving. Chandidasi of the Dome community is a keeper at cemetery, whereas her husband Malindar who has become adept at adapting to the changing times takes up government service. Chandidasi takes up the family's vocation since there is no male member after the death of her father. She traces her lineage to Kalu Dome, the one who protected the mythical King Harischandra when he was ousted from his kingdom. In return for the services the Gangaputta clan was given only the rights to inhabit and the cremation ground. This kind of discrimination since the time of Harischandra is a heavy burden to bear. Malindar, the husband of Chandidasi remarks; "The Brahmins, the sadhus, the sanyasis get cattle, land and gold, and we get all the cremation grounds of the world. All the cremation grounds of the world for us, for us, for us, for us only our mother was a descendent of Kalu Dome. Her name was Chandidasi Gangadasi, she used to bury children" ("Bayen" 79).

Chandidasi is torn between call to take on the ancestral duties and the motherly duty she owes to her only son Bhagirath. She tells Malinder, "It hurts to do the job these days, the job handed down to me by my ancestors, my hands rebel, and yet I have to go on doing it. Can you tell me what I should do? ("Bayen" 82).

Chandidasi's life is made difficult by the superstitious beliefs that are prevalent in her society and she is tormented by the unreasonable behaviour of her husband and relatives. The mental trauma that she is subjected to creates an imbalance which is misidentified by the members of community as 'possession'. She is devastated when her husband refers to her as a 'bayen' and retorts: "What's that you said? So you call me a Bayen? Me, a Bayen? That's what you said, didn't you? So you say I dig up the graves and raise the dead babies? Kiss them? Suckle the dead children? How could you say it?" ("Bayen" 83).

According to Durgesh Ravande, a psychological disorder results from repression caused by the rupture of Chandidasi's motherly ties with her son. Ravande observes, "It stresses also the emotional dynamics related to woman's self-depicted in different cultural situations and concentrates on the feminine disadvantage and lack caused specifically due to repression as a wife or a mother" (202). The father tries to heal the wound inflicted by the loss of mother principle in the son.

**Bhagirath:** My mother? The Bayen's my mother? What sort of a mother?

**Malinder:** You were born of her womb, my son. There was no one as beautiful as she, no one with such a grace.

**Bhagirath;** Then why did you tell me my mother died while I was a baby? Why did you tell me that?

**Malinder:** ...She held you in her womb, she showed you the world, she suckled you, and then she became a Bayen. ("Bayen" 78)

Initially, Chandidasi performed burial rites for children. This is however halted after the government issues a new order which requires that the bodies of children should be cremated and not buried. The family vocation which had sustained the male members of the Dome community becomes a curse when a woman decides to pursue it. Ironically, the earth to which they look to for sustenance becomes the place of defilement or dirt. In this context the dirt theory as proposed by Heather Sullivan in her essay "Dirt Theory and Material Ecocriticism" (2012), is a useful point of reference. According to Sullivan dirt theory is "an antidote to nostalgic views rendering nature a far-away and 'clean' site precisely in order to suggest that there is no ultimate boundary between us and nature. We are enmeshed within dirt in its many forms. Looking at dirty nature allows a close-up and human-scale view of the environment, yet one that is inevitable interconnected with broader views too" ("Dirt Theory and Material Ecocriticism" 515). In Devi's story, the protagonist has an important role to play in the society as the disposer of bodies but at the same time she is despised due to her close association with dirt (dead bodies and the graveyard) considered as pollutants and symbols of inauspiciousness by the society. The local, material environment of Chandidasi, is not accepted by the members of the "mainstream" community. Chandidasi is accused of casting an evil eye on children and she is even blamed for their death, as a result of which she no longer wants to carry on as keeper of the burial ground. She pleads with her husband Malinder that, "Why can't you see it Gangaputta, why I think of throwing up the job again and again? When I guard the graves through the night, my breasts bursting with milk ache for my Bhagirath back home, all by himself. I can't, can't stay away from him." ("Bayen" 82) In her scholarly critique of Mahasweta Devi's mother characters, Radha Chakravorthy remarks that: "Her (Chandi) traditional maternal qualities, such as love, care and protectiveness, are played off against the grotesque, travesty of motherhood that the bayen is supposed to represent" (*Feminism and Contemporary Women Writers* 102). Chandidasi is held responsible for the death of Tukni, the daughter of Pakhi, Malindar's cousin. It is ironic how the community forgets that the child who was nursed by Chandidasi is affected by small pox. After Tukni's death, Chandidasi doesn't perform cremation rites but he guards Tukni's grave from the jackals and other animals. She soliloquises: "There is nothing to be scared of, Tukni dear. I've loved you, little mother of mine, from before the time I had Bhagirath in my womb. It's me on guard, little mother. You needn't be scared. I've planted thorny bushes all round you, the jackals won't come to you, you can be sure" ("Bayen" 85). Being a bayen, she is not killed for the community believes that it would lead to the death of children. She is therefore ostracized and forced to live in a shack with daily belongings being given to her by untouchables. She is disheartened but in the midst of all the troubles she averts a major disaster, a train robbery. She dies in the act of saving the train from looters. Bhagirath, her son summons his courage to tell the world that the courageous lady is none other than his mother Chandidasi. He tells the railway guard: "My name is Bhagirath Gangaputta... My father, the revered Malindar Gangaputta...residence, Domtoli, village Darharhati... My mother... my mother, the late Chandidasi Gangadasi...my mother, the late Chandidasi Gangadasi, sir. Not a Bayen. She was never a Bayen, my mother" ("Bayen" 91).

Mahasweta Devi's "Bayen" invites comparison with the witches in Shakespeare's *Macbeth* (1606) the liminal women, who physically and metaphorically dwell are margin dwellers. Although Chandidasi does not possess supernatural powers like the witches in *Macbeth*, she is ostracized by society as the strange evil woman who has the potential of inflicting harm on unsuspecting targets. In the words of Terry Eagleton, "the witches figure as the 'unconscious' of the drama , of which must be exiled and pressed as dangerous but which is always likely to return with a vengeance" (*William Shakespeare* 47). In a green reading of *Macbeth,* Estok comments on the ecophobia prevalent in the play, "The corporeal norm onto which madness is written as material deformity is gendered, sexualized, classed, and raced. The deforming of this norm tacitly accepts and employs an ecophobic ethic that needs to be addressed if we are to understand how environmentalism... has a vital role to play in liberation movements" (*Ecocriticism and Shakespeare* 100). The term ecophobia was first proposed by Simon Estok in 1995 and it meant, "to denote fear and loathing of the environment" (213). However David Sobel extends this term to include an apprehension towards the disastrous happenings in the world, or rather, "a fear of ecological problems and the natural world" (*Beyond Ecophobia* 5). But ecophobia in this story would mean the act of "imagining badness in nature" (*Beyond Ecophobia* 5) or attributing inauspiciousness to make the audience accept the prevalence of mystery in nature, which is most of the times mystifying to the reader. In Devi's story madness or 'possession' is attributed to the gendered subaltern Chandidasi who becomes a victim of double oppression by both society and culture.

This chapter has attempted to analyse the close connection between women and nature in Devi's fictional narratives and study the manner in which both are 'doubly oppressed.' Although Devi does not claim to be an ecofeminist, her narratives argue in favour of a greater gender inclusiveness regarding women's material position as ecological citizens and the re-valuation of women's work. Like Chandra Talpade Mohanty and Bina Agarwal, Mahasweta Devi too critiques the constructivist glorification of a romanticized vision of poverty and idealization of the Third World Woman. Devi's narratives do not construct the tribal women of India as a homogeneous category but instead draw the reader's attention to other factors like class, caste and several other constituents that make the complex fabric of tribal societies in the modern India. These narratives often disturbingly show how women on account of patriarchal violence have to resort to violent means in order to ensure their survival. Devi's writings have a double focus as Madhu Singh points out: "...in her we find the concrete alternative to resist and destroy not only the injustice of gender politics but also the incursion upon tribal land and forests by feudalism, colonialism and global capitalism" (91). The truth of this statement is embodied in the women characters taken up for analysis in this novel. Mary Oraon resists the capitalist tree felling industry and slays the person who tries to ravage her body. Draupadi asserts her identity as a rebellious woman and protector of the forest, whose body and courage cannot be tarnished by the dastardly rapaciousness of those in power. Dhowli faces rejection by her high-caste lover and his family and is forced by poverty to take to prostitution. Despite this, she emerges a stronger woman who dreams of personhood in a world outside her hierarchy-ridden world. Bayen critiques the ecophobia prevalent in society that leads to the vilification and extreme marginalization of women. The stories "Kunti and Nishadin" and

"Five Women" offer an empowered perspective on womanhood by portraying women as protectors of nature and life. To conclude, these stories which draw from myths as well as socio-political realities offer powerful revisionary narratives which are pluralistic, inclusivist and contextualist.

## Endnote


1. A., Usha. "Feminism in Mahasweta Devi's Selected Stories." *National Journal on Advances in Computing and Management*. Vol. 1.Kodaikanal: 2010. 50-52.
2. Agarwal, Bina. "The Gender and Environment Debate: Lessons from India." *The Women, Gender and Development Reader*. Ed. Nalini Visvanathan, Lynn Duggan, Laurie Nisonoff and Nan Wiegersma. New Delhi: Zubaan, 1997. 68-75.
3. Araya, Karla Araya. "The case of Mary's identity as a reversal of gender roles in Devi Mahasweta's "The Hunt"." *Comunicación,* Vol 19. Cost Rica: Instituto Tecnológico de Costa Rica, 52-55.
4. Baviskar, Amita. "Tribal Politics and Discourses of Indian Environmentalism." *Nature in the Global South: Environmental Projects in South and Southeast Asia*. Ed. Paul Greenough and Anna Lowenhaupt Tsing. USA: Duke University Press,2003. 289-318.
5. Beniwal, Anup and Vandana. "Writing the Subaltern at the Interface of Fiction and Ideology: an engagement in the works of Mahasweta Devi." *New Quest*165-166. 2006. 84-92.
6. Bhabha, Homi J. *The Location of Culture*. London: Routledge, 1994.
7. Chakravarty, Radha. "Visionary Cartography: *Imaginary Maps* by *Mahasweta Devi An Anthology of Recent Criticism.* Ed. Nivedita Sen and Nikhil Yadav. New Delhi. Pencraft International. 2008. 190-203.
8. Devi, Mahasweta. "The Hunt." *Imaginary Maps*. Trans. Gayatri Spivak. New York: Routledge, 1995. 1-18.
9. —"Doulati the Bountiful." *Imaginary Maps*. Trans. Gayatri Spivak. New York: Routledge, 1995.19-94.
10. —"Dhowli." *Of Women, Outcastes, Peasants, and Rebels: A Selection of Bengali Short Stories*. Ed. Kalpana Bardhan. California: University of California Press, 1990. 185-205.

11. – "Five Women." *After Kurukshetra*. Trans. Anjum Katyal. Kolkata: Seagull Books, 2005. 1-22.
12. –"Kunti and Nishadin." *After Kurukshetra*. Trans Anjum Katyal. Kolkata: Seagull Books, 2005.
13. –"Draupadi." *Critical Inquiry*. Trans. Gayatri Spivak. *Critical Inquiry*. Trans. Gayatri Spivak. Vol. 8, No. 2, University of Chicago, 1981.381-402.
14. –. *Five Plays*.trans. Samik Bandyopadhyay. Calcutta: Seagull Books,1997.
15. Estok, Simon. *Ecocriticism and Shakespeare: Reading Ecophobia: Literatures, Cultures, and the Environment*. New York: Palgrave Macmillan, 2011. 1-100.
16. Jaidev, S. "Doulati as a National Allegory." *Mahasweta Devi An Anthology of Recent Criticism*. Ed. Nivedita Sen and Nikhil Yadav.New Delhi. Pencraft International. 2008.86-102.
17. Karunanayake, Dinithi. "Dismantling Theory? Agency and the Subaltern Woman in Mahasweta Devi's Draupadi". "Colombo: University of Colombo, 2008.
18. Kheel, Marti. "Finding a Niche for All Animals in Nature Ethics." *Nature Ethics: An Ecofeminist Perspective*. Maryland: Rowman and Littlefield Publishers, 2008.1-34.
19. King, Ynestra."The Ecology of Feminsm and the Feminism of Ecology." *Healing the Wounds: The Promise of Ecofeminsm*. Ed. Judith Plant. Philadelphia: New Society Publishers, 1989.106-120.
20. Lutgendorf, Philip. "City, Forest, and Cosmos: Ecological Perspectives from the Sanskrit Epics." *Hinduism and Ecology*. Ed. Christopher Key Chapple and Mary Evelyn Tucker. Harvard: Harvard University Press, 2000. 269-278.
21. Martinez, Juan Alier. *The Environmentalism of the Poor: A Study of Ecological Conflicts and Valuation*. Massachusetts: Edward Elgar Publishing,2002. 1-16.
22. Merchant, Carolyn. *Reinventing Eden: The Fate of Nature in Western Culture*. 2nd ed. New York: Routledge, 2013.1-8.
23. Oster, Laura Hobgood. "Ecofeminism: Historic and International Evolution." *The Encyclopaedia of Religion and Nature*. Vol. 2. Ed. Bron Taylor. London: Continuum Books, 2005. 534-539.
24. Panikkar, Raimundo. *Myth, Faith and Hermeneutics*. Bangalore: Asian Trading Association.1983 300-500.
25. Plumwood, Val. *Feminism and Mastery of Nature*. New York: Routledge, 1993. 1-18., Print.
26. Raman, Sita Anantha. "Region, Environment, Gender."

*Women in India: A Social and Cultural History*. Vol. 1. California: Prager, 2009. 1-15.

27. Rangarajan, Swarnalatha. "Writing as Mukti: The Story of Draupadi, the Subaltern who Speaks." *Voices of the Voiceless: Perspectives on Subaltern Literatures*. Ed. Francis Peter Chennai: ACE-Loyola, 2003. 87-94.
28. Reuther, Rosemary Radford. *Womanguides: Readings Toward a Feminist Theology*. Boston: Beacon Press, 1985.65-67.
29. Schweitzer, Albert. "Reverence for Life." *Civilization and Ethics*. London: Adams and Charles Black, 1923.
30. Shiva, Vandana. "Development, Ecology and Women." *Staying Alive: Women, Ecology and Survival in India*. New Delhi: Kali for Women, 1988. xiv-15. Print.
31. Singh, Madhu. "Nature and nurture in Mahasweta Devi's Dystopia: A Study of Mahdu: A Fairytale." Vol. 1. New Delhi: Indian Journals, 2004. Web.
32. Starhawk. *The Fifth Sacred Thing*. New York: Bantam Publishers, 1993. Print.
33. Sullivan, Heather I. "Dirt Theory and Material Ecocriticism." *ISLE*. Vol 19. Oxford: Oxford Journals, 2012. 515-531.
34. Sobel, David. *Beyond Ecophobia: Reclaiming the Heart in Nature Education*. Great Barrington: Orion Press, 1994.
35. Tharu, Susie J., and K. Lalita. *Women Writing in India: The Twentieth Century*. Vol. II. New York: The Feminist Press, 1993. 235-250.
36. Warren, Karen J. "The Power and the Promise of Ecological Feminism." *Environmental Ethics*. Vol. 12. Ed. David R. Keller. Oxford: Wiley Blackwell Publishers, 1990. 125-133.
37. Wenzel, Jennifer. "Forest Fictions and Ecological Crises: Reading the Politics of Survival in Mahasweta Devi's "Dhowli"." *Postcolonial Ecologies*. Ed. Elizabeth De Loughrey and George Handley. Oxford: Oxford University Press, 2011. 136-157.

# Environmental Art Challenging the Tradition of Landscape Painting : A Contemporary Study

**Juhi Latwal Mehra**

## Introduction

Environmental art is a crucial issue, which is also addressed as Ecology art. Environmental art is often discussed in the context of Anglo-American art.[1] Different styles, forms, and expressions altogether created an art movement which was called Land art. In Land art or Earthwork, artists use natural assets or the natural environment as material for their artwork. Earth art physically interacts with the landscape; it cannot be ecologically natural.[2,3] This art movement emerged in 1960 in the USA.[4] "Environmentalism" term was used dominantly since the 1970s which refers to the social movement motivated by Sundry for concern related to the preservation and protection of the environment.[5] Environmental art is about man and nature's relationship, and when we talk about nature or artwork inspired by nature the very first thing that strikes our mind is "landscape painting". Art or art piece is the visual galleries that help us understand that nature is not an eternal circle in harmony, but has mortal existence in history which is irreversible in time just like human beings.[6] Environmental artists are raising issues on the deterioration of the environment which is speeding up every minute and is further elevating other issues such as global warming, famine, causing danger to species, etc. Environments are not physical places but perceptual ones, that we collaborate in making, and it is perceptually that we determine their identity and extent (Berleant 1992, 155)[7]. This perceptual ability of nature has inspired artists through ages.

In the present scenario, the definition of landscape in visual art is incompatible with Renaissance and Impressionism periods. Presently it is seen as material rather than subject and artists expression of nature observation. Modes like installation, sculptures, photography, etc. are used to express the concept and demonstrate the issues with a creative approach, which soar as a new methodology for environmental education. The environment has been symbolized as emotions, the cycle of life in many cultures. Asian art and artists have personified nature and natural elements in their art which can be traced later in western art. This article is focused on the philosophical approach and materials used by artists in their artwork where they have illustrated nature from subject to material. The nature as material rather than the subject has made difference visually in art, concept, and time.

## Nature in Early Phase of Art

Prehistoric art can be called a rudimentary endeavour to depict nature, which was further cultivated subsequently. Folk art all over the world contains natural elements like trees, rivers, mountains, animals, etc. that which are inspired by mythology. Nature, the only source of life is personified in Asian art. Here, nature was identified as a powerful God or individual who possesses the power to destroy and create. Landscape painting is a reflection of our actions where we witness the destruction and harm, we have caused to nature by dragging it down from a powerful individual (where it was worshiped as God) to a pitiful victim. In the early phase of the art, we will be focused on the depiction of nature in Indian art, focused on the Mughal era of "Jahangir" and Chinese landscape which were purely devoted to nature.

In the early sixteen-century painting, there were strong interests in the flora and fauna of India.[8] Mughal era was dedicated to nature and reached sky high in the Jahangir period. The well-known Hamza Nama folios from around 1556 to 1565 are filled with flowers, various fowl, forests, and verdant settings.[9] In this phase of the art, artists were mesmerized by nature's beauty and were in quest of creating an accurate artistic impression of the same. Although Hamza Nama depicts motifs that lack flora decoration as they were highly inspired by Persian and Turkish art. Jahangir Era is marked as a golden period, when Mughal decorative art bloomed fully from, creative expression featuring abundant floral imaginary.[10] Every artifact – dagger, vessels, jade, etc., was filled with motifs that were full of natural inspiration. Kashmir landscape and representation of flowers greatly increased in Jahangir painting and decorative objects.[11] Artist of that era was mesmerized and bewitched by nature that they couldn't help depicting it.

The initial phase in Asian art was dominated by religious philosophy which was deeply rooted in Asia art. The word "chi" designates Chinese philosophy which is the base of their art. Chinese landscape painting is a projection in the Visual terms of Chinese philosophy, or of the Chinese mind.[12] *Shan-Sui* is a Chinese term used for landscape painting that on leans "mountain and river",which symbolize opposite force. It is the way to depict Yang, Ying, their interplay, and their unity at a higher level.[13] The philosophy of opposite force and erection of Universe through their union is the base of religious philosophy which was embraced in painting. Chinese landscape art is the reflection of nature's soul, for creating a painting with powerful and incredible expression that artists try to connect their soul with nature's soul"- Chi". Therefore, landscape painting is regarded as the highest painting according to the Chinese principle of art.

Both Indian and Chinese paintings principles are rooted deep in nature, which symbolizes life. As mentioned above, these periods of painting are not only about movement but the intensity of nature. Natural assets like Nagas, Himalaya, rivers, Therianthrope, Peepal tree, etc. are personified almost in every religion to signify human emotions. For example-mountains occupy an important place in Hindu Mythology as a symbol of strength[14] Similarly, a bull symbolized Shiva, Sarasvati is celebrated as a purifying, fertilizing, enriching power[15] and etc. many more. It will be totally unfair to say that the artists perception was limited till aesthetic pleasure. Art, predominantly landscape painting, delineates nature in its different shades. For example, the Impressionism period in the western landscape was the interplay of light and shades, whereas Chinese landscape apart from "Chi" emphasises on birds-eye view or aerial perspective. On the other hand, Indian landscape were full of nativeness and essence of *Rasa*. Later these concepts were reconstructed with contemporary environment and elements.

## Animism in Contemporary Art

Art has always played an important role as a reformer and has modelled itself as per the environment. These changes are not only seen in the subject selection but the material choices too. Paper as canvases have almost lost their identity as a convenient material for artistic expression. Artists today are working beyond boundaries and are using natural assets as material. Limning hot issues with this approach are spellbinding masses and critics. Worldwide, many articles, publications, and seminars are conducted where scholars have persuaded their opinion on Environmental art. Most of this attention has been focused on evaluating the ethical and aesthetical quality of art objects[16] "Is Environment Art an Aesthetic Affront of Nature?", an article by Allen Carlson[17] is the most provocative and discussed article. But in this paper, we focus on the artists and their artwork who are working as environmental activists. Installation, sculpture, architect model and Graffiti are modes used by these activists.

Roadsworth graffiti street artist, also known as Peter Gibson, whose stencil style which is characterized as inherently political because its transformative power that is seen to be embodied in its aesthetic forms[18,19] The 9/11 incident left a deep impression on him after which he used the city space of Montreal as the canvas[20] His artwork is based on environmental issues like- excess gasoline and electricity use, lack of wildlife, etc. For executing his idea, he has made use of public space and twisted them into a canvas. He often turns pedestrian walkways into large footprints (see fig-2), parking lots into flowers (see fig-.3), traffic lines into electrical cords and fishing lines, and crosswalks into images of electrical switches[21]

Fig. -1

Fig. -2

Fig.-3

Agnes Denes is a sculptor, environmental installer, who is well known for her Wheatfield installation - *A Confrontation* (1982), (see fig.-4). The misuse of land or abuse of space[22] is the concept of her installation. This installation diverts our mind to other issues which are raised from misusing land such as famine, endangered wildlife, deforestation, water, etc. She herself cleared that she does not want to raise her voice for the world hunger, and the end of many things[23] as many others have done that. In her interview with Gabrielle Schwarz, she said- my work deals with problems humanity have and is trying to find a benign solution"[24] This installation is planted on two acres and is funded by public art. According to artists, her installations are above philosophy and aesthetics and are aimed at humanity. She is working on many other projects which are inspired and dedicated to nature. A virgin forest is one of her projects, also known as *Tree Mountain*, 1992, Future city projects are those projects which help humans realize the importance of natural sources and how to deal with the destruction of the environment caused by humans.

Fig.-4 a

Fig-4 b

Martha Thoma created a sculpture named *"Earth Tear"* which was constructed by using plastic bottles. Thoma's *Earth Tear* is a sculpture that is 8 feet tall and is built by using 250 plastic bottles. This sculpture was created during a residential artists' program. The process and intention behind this sculpture were to evaluate the learning process and the sensitivity of students towards the Environment (as it was an experiment). Mathilde Roussel, a French artist, has created a series of green human figures in her installation is known as *green living sculpture* (see fig. 5). Recycled materials, soil and seeds are used for installation. The concept of the installation is the "centrality of food"[25] This installation diverts our mind towards the sensitive and current issues of the food cycle, the suffering of creatures all over the world due to insufficient supplies, and the degradation of nature. Paulo Grangeon, a French Sculptor installed 1,600 paper-mache bears in 2008 which was called *"Pandas on Tour"* (see fig. 6). The artist's motto was to support and arouse awareness about the endangered species which is the result of environmental disbalance caused by misusing and abusing resources. The actual number of Pandas (survived on earth) was used to make the concept impactful and direct us towards deforestation and global warming problems. Amanda Schachter and Alexander Levi are two architects who have created a masterpiece by using umbrellas and plastic bottles (see fig.-7). Such creative ideas can help us deal with piles of garbage in creative and useful ways. Further development in such ideas can help us in overcoming flood and earthquake destruction as these types of construction would avoid further destruction of nature and life while preventing the misuse of land.

Fig.-5

Fig-6

Fig-7

In mass opinion, Nature is depicted or represented in art for aesthetic purposes alone. Presently this viewpoint has been demolished by an extensive change in the approach and treatment of artistic work. In the present scenario, artists raise the issue of the environment with innovative ideas and modes. Naziha Mestaoui came up with the idea of "one beat one tree" which is a digital art project that innovatively focuses on deforestation issues. In this project, there are two trees one is virtual and the other is physical. The person who is part of this project can connect him/her with their virtual tree and can witness the growth of the same in the form of a heartbeat. This is how activist art is motivating and inspiring an individual to protect the environment worldwide. Visual art has always played an important role in exploring and exposing issues. Environmental artists have put their best to attract people's attention towards environmental issues and come up with projects installations most of which are not aesthetically but are also economically beneficial such as the Agnes -Wheatfield installation.

Contemporary art and issues portrayed by artists reflect our relationship with nature and how the aesthetic value of nature is constantly changed from subject to material. Artists have risen as an activist than an appreciator. Such art movement is allied with different art forms, which are raising their voice and artists are working as environmental artists or Earth/Land artists. Environmental art has developed a characteristic termed as "site-specific."[26] Being site-specific means that art also serves as a mnemonic device for the narrative[27]. Itoh Takako in her article "Historization of Nature -Narrative of British Environmental Art", has examined the installation of two British artists who are environmentalists and their works are inspired by the historical background of the site. "Ash-Dome" by David Nash is a sculpture made by living trees for this artist planted ash tree seedlings in 1997. The concept of this installation was very clear that only the collaboration of nature can realize sustainable human life[28] People often find it difficult to understand environmental art as art because of their idealism and lack of landscape narrative can be coded in the early phase of art. Thus, environmental art is conflated and complicates "art" and "nature", because it directly makes use of the natural environment in its artistic realization[29].

## Reference


1. Takako Itoh, Debating Ethical Issues Surrounding Environmental art: On "Is Environmental Art an Aesthetic Affront to Nature? published in Japanese Society of Aesthetics, Aesthetics No.25 (2021): 51-62.
2. cited by Ibid-1.
3. Auping Michael, "Earth Art: A Study in Ecological Politics ", in Alan Sonfist (ed.) Art in the Land, A critical Anthology of Environmental Art, 1983, p.34.
4. Ibid-1.
5. Grey William, Environmentalism, unpublished paper, The University of Queensland, Australia.
6. Takako Itoh, Historization of nature-Narrative of British Environmental Art, Journal of International Philosophy No.2 2013.
7. Jokela Timo, From Environmental art to Environmental Education, M.H Ed. 1995, the image of Earth: Writing on art-based environmental education. (pp.18-28), Helsinki, Finland: University of Art and Design.
8. Markel Stephen, The use of Flora and Fauna Imagery In Mughal Decorative Arts, edited by S.P Verma, Mumbai Marg publications,1999, pp 25-35.
9. Ibid-8.
10. Ibid-8.
11. Ibid-8.
12. Briessen Van Fritz, The Way of The Brush, Published by The Charles E. Tuttle. Co. of Rutland Vermont and Tokyo Japan, Library of Congress Catalog Card no. 62-14119,1962, page no.-78.

13. Ibid- 1, page no.- 79.
14. Ions Veronica, Indian Mythology, published by Paul Hamlyn London,1967, page no.107.
15. Ibid-4, Page No.- 89.
16. Simus Jason, Environmental Art, and Ecological Citizenship, spring 2008, page no.-21.
17. Ibid-1.
18. Cited by Truman J. Emily in-The (In) Visible Artist: Stencil Graffiti, Activist Art, and the value of Visual Public Space, SHIFT- Queens Journal of Visual and Material Culture, Issue 3,2010.
19. Cited from Guido Indij, 1000 Stencil: Argentina graffiti, (Buenos Aeries: La Marca Editora,2007),228.
20. Ibid- 18.
21. Ibid-18.
22. Schwarz Gabrielle, "My Art Is About Overcoming Our Limitation"-an interview with Agnes Denes, Apollo, International Art Magazine,11 Oct -2019.
23. Ibid-22.
24. Ibid-22.
25. Brooks Katherine, Cultures and Arts, 18 green artists that are making climate change and conservation a priority, 7/15/2014(Huff post).
26. Ibid-6.
27. Ibid-6
28. Ibid-6.
29. Ibid-6.

❑❑